# *LIFTING* the *WAIT*

## A STORY ABOUT FAITH, FITNESS & PERFECT TIMING

# ATHENA PEREZ

# LIFTING THE WAIT

**Editors:**
Andréa Maria Cecil Topper
Patti Bond

**Cover Design:**
Lance Buckley
www.lancebuckley.com

**Interior Design:**
Brooklyn Taylor
www.brooktown.com

**Cover Photography:**
Chris Pulliam
www.cpullphotos.com

Roxanne Rhodes
www.roxymichellephotography.com

Printed in the United States of America

ASIN: B089NZ8ZCX

Disclaimer: This book is about Athena Perez's life, a combination of facts and certain embellishments. The author recognizes that her memories of the events she described may be different from the people described in the book. Some names, dates, places, events and details have been changed, invented and altered for literary effect. Some names and identifying details of certain individuals have been changed to protect their privacy. The chronology of some events has been compressed. Some conversations have been recreated and/or supplemented. The reader should not consider this book anything other than a work of literature. The information in this book is not advice and should not be treated as such. Do not substitute this information for the medical advice of physicians. Always consult your doctor for your individual needs. Consult a physician for matters relating to your physical health or mental health and any symptoms that may require diagnosis or medical attention.

Published by Eagle Rise Publishing, Virginia Beach, VA www.EagleRisePublishing.com

# ACKNOWLEDGMENTS

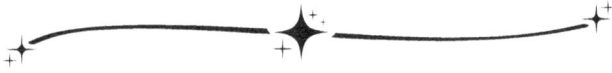

Above all else, I am genuinely grateful to God and His Son, Jesus Christ. I am truly blessed. With all that I am, I thank you today for all you do every day.

*I will praise you, Lord, with all my heart; I will tell of all the marvelous things you have done* -- Psalm 9:1.

For my dearly loved parents, Anthony and Melody, for supporting my dreams, championing my projects and encouraging my pursuits.

To my siblings Noel, Kim, Jay, Luke, Aaron, Colin and Barrett: I love you guys so much.

Most profound appreciation to the selfless therapist, friend and spiritual mentor that worked countless hours to help me heal so I could function with dignity and respect.

Thank you, divine universe, for letting there be 80s music, coffee and dogs.

To my closest friend, Dennis, for being there for me through every tear and every laugh. I love you.

Special recognition to Mike Koslap, Tyson Oldroyd, Sevan Matossian, Rory McKernan and the CrossFit® community at large for its endless supply of support, messages of encouragement, high fives and burpees. Yes, even burpees. Without all of you, this book would not have been possible.

To my superheroes who truly inspire me: Cole Sager, Rich Froning, Chris Spealler, Dan Bailey, Noah Ohlsen and Tasia Percevecz.

Writing a book is a surreal and humbling process. I am forever indebted to Andréa Maria Cecil Topper for her editorial help, keen insight and ongoing support in bringing my story to life.

And finally, to all of the great authors and mentors who have impacted my life so profoundly, including the one, specifically, who inspired me to write this book: Greg Amundson.

# CONTRIBUTORS

At the end of every chapter there is a lesson or takeaway.

These thoughts were collaborations with some of my favorite friends, superheroes and people I admire. I value and respect each of them for inspiring me and contributing to my life in some way. I would like to recognize them with sincere appreciation for their willingness to donate their time, energy and support. I am blessed and truly grateful for their thoughts and genuine perspective. All of our stories are different, but what we share in common is the true human experience: Life.

*Tasia Percevecz*
—@tasiapercevecz on Instagram

*Dave Eubanks*
—@cfeubanks on Instagram

*Chase Knight*
—@coach_chase_cfl2 on Instagram

*Rory McKernan*
—@rorymckernan on Instagram

*Tyson Oldroyd*
—@tysonold on Instagram

*Mike Koslap*
—@mikekoslap on Instagram

*Sara Krych*
—@sarakrych on Instagram

*Al Sagapolutele*
—@sagapolutele_al on Instagram

*Jennifer Pendleton*
—@jenxjourney on Instagram

**Justin Gehrt**
—@justingehrt on Instagram

# DEDICATION

In memory of Owen Abner and Aidan Stone

# CONTENTS

# FOREWORD BY GREG AMUNDSON

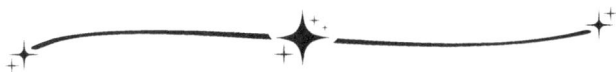

IN DECEMBER 2001, I WALKED INTO A SMALL CrossFit® Box, experienced the thrill of my first workout, crumbled into a heap on the floor, and thought that I was going to die. Since that fateful encounter nearly 20 years ago, six days a week have been committed to CrossFit — the seventh is set apart for Church. Sunday has always been my day of Sabbath rest onto the Lord.

This is precisely why on the morning of Sunday, July 1, 2018, it came as such a puzzling surprise when I strongly felt the Holy Spirit gently nudge me to go to my CrossFit gym.

"But Sundays are my rest day!" I protested. Although my condo was only a short three-minute Santa Cruz flip-flop away from my gym on 38th Avenue, the thought of breaking the rhythm and pattern of my Sabbath seemed blasphemous. However, if there's one thing I've learned in my walk with the Lord it's this: Obedience brings blessing — and perfect obedience brings miracles.

A few minutes later I walked through the doors of CrossFit Amundson and came face to face with the grace-filled, beautiful, smiling face of Athena Perez — the woman who would teach me more about faith, obedience, and perfect timing than anyone I've ever known. As it turned out, Athena had strongly felt God leading her to my studio on that exact same morning — and at the exact same time.

The Bible says, "The steps of a righteous person are ordered by the LORD" (Psalm 37:23). I love this verse because of the way it has consistently proven itself true in my life. Although I don't profess to always understand God — I do profess that I trust Him.

Athena reminds me of Abraham, the great biblical hero of faith. The Scripture teaches, "By faith Abraham, when called to go to a place he would later receive as his inheritance, obeyed and went, even though he did not know where he was going" (Hebrews 11:8).

*By faith.*

*Abraham obeyed God and went.*

*Even though Abraham did not know exactly where he was going.*

In many respects, this verse encapsulates Athena's brilliant new book, LIFTING the WAIT. I believe that many people never realize their full potential and fulfill their life purpose because they lack the faith to wait on God to lead them into the great unknown. In other words, trusting in God and waiting on God are two sides of the same coin.

In the few years that I've known Athena, she's made a tremendous imprint on my life. She makes me laugh one moment, and cry the next. She inspires me to help others, and to ask for help when I need it. She teaches me to set big goals, and to have the wisdom to let things go.

Most importantly, through every lesson, Athena helps me see that God is with us, He is for us, and He will do whatever it takes to reconcile ourselves to Him.

Athena's book is a masterpiece. I pray that her words will bless your life.

Shalom,

~ *Greg Amundson*, CrossFit's "Original Firebreather" and #1 bestselling author of *The Warrior and The Monk*

# INTRODUCTION

My name is Athena. Most of my family and dearest friends call me "Bean," a nickname I got when I was just a baby. Hearing it used to make my eyes roll when I was kid. I couldn't stand it. But it grew on me. I eventually learned to embrace my nickname. Today, my 12 nieces and nephews know me as "Auntie Bean."

I live north of Saint Paul, Minnesota, in a quiet suburb with my two dogs Poppy and Kodiak.

I consider myself a proud Christian. But it wasn't always this way. For most of my life, I believed there was a God, but I didn't always have the best relationship with Him.

I spent most of my childhood and well into my 30s believing bad things happen to good people and that life was one big coincidence. Either we got lucky and had great circumstances or we got the short end of the stick.

There were times when I even believed God might have a sense of humor. After all, some of the things I had experienced in life reminded me of soap operas and daytime television. What if God was up there just throwing stuff in the mix and watching all of us fumble and freak out for entertainment? I considered the possibility that maybe this was reality. What other explanation could there be? Despite believing he was a comic, I still wanted to believe in Him. That's why I continued to pray all of those times when I needed help. Most of the time, I felt like I was doing it for nothing. He was never going to show up. He was never going to help me. He was never going to take the pain away. So, why did I do it? I felt like it was nothing more than a waste of time.

I remember getting on my knees as a child and praying for the mental and physical abuse to stop. God never came. In my teens, I prayed for my father to love me. God never answered. In my 20s when I went through one tragic event after another, where was God? He was not there. My prayers were never answered, and he certainly wasn't calling me on my cell to have a chat. In my 30s, when I was on the brink of suicide and I had no reason to continue living, where was God? Time and time again I felt ignored. I resigned myself to the belief that I was the child God forgot.

Until it all changed. All of it.

How did I get here? How did I go from believing the act of prayer and God himself were jokes, to a place where I would be excited to share God with others? I experienced something so powerful it could only have come from God. My life changed when I realized my prayers — every single one of them — were being answered all along. God hadn't forgotten about me. His hand was in every request. How could I not have seen?

★   ★   ★

In April 2018, I received an email asking if I would like to come to California the next month to be on the CrossFit Inc. podcast. I was shocked. I had thought the podcast was reserved for elite athletes. I certainly was not one of those. I knew very few names of the elite and I had never been to the CrossFit Games. In fact, when I received the podcast invite, I didn't know the hosts. I was just an ordinary woman with zero elite athletic skills.

CrossFit was not a sport to me; it was a tool I was using to combat severe morbid obesity. I couldn't run that far due to severe degradation in my knees. I couldn't do muscle-ups or handstand walks. What was I going to do in California, sitting in the same chair as Games competitors Dan Bailey, Brooke Ence and Mat Fraser?

The podcast invite was intended to follow up an April 2018 CrossFit Journal video about my 200 pound weight loss journey. My world, as I knew it, changed the very day that Journal story hit CrossFit's social media platforms.

I was getting hundreds of messages every day. I would spend my entire lunch hour and most of my evening at my computer trying to respond to every kind soul who had sent me well wishes or messages of encouragement. I was exhausted but trying to continue going to my 5:30 a.m. CrossFit class that had me in bed no later than 8:30 p.m. That didn't include trying to respond to every comment. I was getting lost in the abyss of Instagram, Facebook and YouTube. I finally gave up trying to respond to every person and decided I would do my absolute best, though this still was difficult. Would all of these people know how grateful I was?

The podcast, itself, was an experience. I was nervous because a week earlier I listened to every episode I could squeeze into my day. The host, Sevan Matossian, had a direct and blunt approach. In my video, I shared a snippet of some of my dark days from the past so I knew this would probably be a topic they wanted to cover. I was not just going to have to share a snippet of my past; I was going to have to share all of it.

But what I experienced was not what I had seen in previous podcasts. Sevan was gentle and genuinely curious about my history. There was something about him that I was drawn to almost immediately. Although I was still nervous during the interview, I felt calm with him and his questions. It wasn't the questions that made me nervous, it was the multiple cameras that had never been in my face before.

As I was staring out the window on my flight home, I felt like there was something I needed to do. I received a prompt that I needed to write. Sometimes prompts come from little voices in my head that just won't be quiet. **This prompt was so loud** I couldn't ignore it. I had a story to tell; I needed to get it on paper. It wasn't just an idea I had been kicking around for a few months, I almost felt like the heavens were handing me a school assignment. I had learned to listen to those prompts; I trusted them explicitly. But this time, they were asking for more.

Initially, I had a problem with the voice. It said, "Athena, quit your job and write."

The first problem: I was not a writer. I mean, sure, I blogged, but I had never written a book. I was not an English major, I never studied journalism, or anything closely related. I didn't even use proper grammar when I wrote emails. I didn't know the first thing about what went into writing a book.

The second problem: I still had a mortgage, a car payment and other bills to pay.

Still, I listened, and quit my job six weeks later.

The following month, things became clearer.

During the last week of June, I made the trek back to California for the CrossFit Level 1 Certificate Course in Aromas. The take-aways were terrific and life-changing, but I still hadn't made much progress on writing. By this time, weeks had gone by since my last day at work. On the second day of the course, I was physically exhausted and also frustrated by my lack of direction for the book. I decided it was time to pray again and give my stress, doubts and worries to God and see what happened.

"God, I listened to you and I am writing, but I don't know how to tell any of this. This is too hard. I can't do it."

The following morning, I awoke at 6:30 a.m. My body was screaming at me in the shower from slinging a nearly weightless PVC pipe around all weekend at the Level 1 course, but the warm water on my legs felt good. As I rinsed the conditioner out of my hair, I got a strange thought: "I need to go to Greg Amundson's gym."

Where was this coming from? I didn't know that much about him. How did I even know Amundson's gym was in Santa Cruz?

In true Athena fashion — as I had done so many times before in the previous 18 months — I listened to the voice. Still, I felt frustrated. What was going to happen once I got to Amundson's gym? Nevertheless, I got dressed, packed up and checked out of the hotel. It was 8:10 a.m.

I arrived at Amundson CrossFit at around 8:45 a.m. and immediately saw two faces I recognized from my Level 1 course. What a pleasant surprise! I ended up talking to one of these gentlemen for quite some time as I explained some of my story and what I was doing in California. He mentioned, "Hey, you should come back this evening. Coach will be here, and you can meet him." I explained that my flight was leaving at 2 p.m., and, sadly, I wouldn't be able to make that work. No less than 5 minutes later, Greg Amundson strolled into the gym.

It was a surprise.

I wasn't counting on being able to meet Greg, and, to be honest, expected nothing. But this warm, kind man took the time to talk to me, learn about me and ended up giving me a signed copy of his book.

A few hours later, I am impatiently listening to the flight attendant rattle off the safety card information. As soon as the voice on the loudspeaker stopped, I dove into the book, "The Warrior and the Monk: A Fable About Fulfilling Your Potential And Finding True Happiness." Shortly before the four-hour flight arrived in Minneapolis I finished the short but impactful read. It was a "delightful tale about a young warrior who seeks the counsel of a wise monk on a universal quest to find true happiness." At various points of the read, I found myself getting teary-eyed. There was a reason I ran into Greg that morning, and there was a reason he gave me a copy of his book. I felt as if I had just read my own story. This book was not just a fable; it's a real story that happens in real life. It happened to me.

I had a sudden realization that what I needed to share in my book was the journey itself because that was where I found my answers. Nothing that had happened in my life was a coincidence, and it certainly didn't mean I got the short end of the stick. Just because things in my life were surprising to me doesn't mean they were unexpected to God.

It states in the Bible in Matthew 10:29 that if God tracks every sparrow, then nothing is too small for his attention. In ways unknown to me, he took all of my hurt and all of those unplanned events and wove them together to fulfill His purpose.

My weight loss success was only a fraction of the story. I don't even believe it is the story anymore. The story is not about me losing weight or lifting weights. It's about how I lifted the wait.

# CHAPTER 1:

## *STOP. JUST STOP*

I didn't know much about Minnesota the year I decided to visit in the summer of 2007.

I had been living in Texas for nine years and did a lot of traveling, but never to the Midwest. I knew Minnesotans had harsh winters, loved hockey and had a massive mall called "Mall of America." That was the extent of my knowledge.

I had no specific plans other than a quick weekend away from the Texas heat and monotony of my senior year in college. From the moment my plane landed, I felt something magical I couldn't explain if I tried. It was as if it felt like home. There was lots of water, big evergreen trees and quaint craftsman-style houses with tree-lined streets that reminded me of a post-card. I loved the Minnesota accent, it was quirky, distinct and endearing. I fell in love in a matter of three short days; in fact, I was so excited about it, I immediately went back to Texas and announced to my then fiancé Nick that if we ever left Texas we should move to Minnesota.

Nick was not quite as excited about my discovery. To say he believed I had lost all common sense might have been the understatement of the year. My idea slowly rolled off like a tumbleweed. Looking back, I didn't understand how powerful our intentions are, and that the things we think about, we bring about.

★   ★   ★

Two years later, it was a windy evening in South Texas in November 2009. My eyes were so puffy I could hardly open them, but I could hear the windchimes banging against the back-glass door. I had cried to the point they were sore, and my wet cheeks were raw. I knew I wanted to pray, but I hadn't been on my knees to pray since I was a child. God had ignored me back then. Why would this prayer be any different?

I hobbled into my bathroom, and with tears still running down my face and snot coming out of my nose, I pulled open the bathroom medicine cabinet. I fumbled with the bottles, moving various pills around until I thought I had found the three most potent potions in the cupboard. Now, how many pills would it take? I had a gun in my nightstand drawer, but the thought of my parents finding me with a bullet in my head made me cry harder. How could I do that to them?

Furthermore, how had it become so bad that I was contemplating suicide in the first place? I couldn't allow my loving mother and stepfather to find me dead in my room. I screamed in frustration and threw the bottles at my wall; the pills came crashing out of their containers and landed all over my bedroom floor.

I sank to the floor, weeping in agony.

"God...are you there?"

I don't know for sure how long I was crying and talking out loud to the God I swore was going to ignore me anyway. Did I think he'd listen? No, I didn't. But I had nowhere else to go at that exact moment.

I knew I needed help, but I didn't know what kind. I needed a different life, and I wanted to be a different person. Seemingly, my life felt like one adverse event after another, and it just kept sucking me in with no way out. I wanted it to STOP. The life I knew up to that point had made me angry, bitter, resentful and cold. I wanted a life less complicated. No more lawsuits, no more court cases, no more staying with someone because I felt stuck and worthless. I prayed to God I could feel peace, something I don't think I had ever felt in my 32 years of living.

I woke up the next morning, still on the floor. I must have talked to God until I fell asleep because there I was looking up at the ceiling while my dog sniffed my hair and face. A part of me believed that spilling my guts out to God was futile, but admittedly, I did feel better. I couldn't see the horizon in front of me, but I still had hope and a sense of knowing. I didn't know what, but it didn't take that long to find out.

12 hours after I managed to pull myself off the bedroom floor, I had the most random encounter on Facebook with a high school-aged kid named Dennis. He was passionate about graphic design and wanting assistance with starting up a clothing brand for young skateboarders and snowboard-ers. I was inspired by his passion and felt the designs were oddly entertaining. I felt so low in my own life and had many regrets. I was in a relationship that I felt stuck in and nothing got me excited to wake up in the morning. How many kids that age put a wish or desire out there on the internet and actually have someone respond and say, "Yeah, I would be willing to help." I wanted to be that person. Initially I thought I would just supply the financial backing and watch him grow; I didn't exactly plan on getting involved in the business. I didn't know anything about building a clothing brand from scratch. Hell, I had never snowboarded or skateboarded in my life. But...I learned how to create quickly.

I spent what seemed like hundreds of hours learning how to communicate with technical clothing designers and watched in awe when a simple idea became something tangible on a design card. We studied and learned the manufacturing process, learned how to select yarns, fabrics, patterns, and interpretation of technical drawings. It's incredible how fast it happened; it was almost overnight. I was living in Texas; Dennis was in Minnesota and we communicated via phone and email getting this tiny clothing brand off the ground. It was something so unlike anything I had ever done, but for the first time in my life, I felt happy. I was working probably 10-12 hours a day on the business on top of working a business I already owned, but it really didn't feel like work. Aside from the joy it brought me, there was an irony in meeting Dennis as he was from Minnesota. Of all the millions of places he could have been from, he was from Minnesota.

★   ★   ★

10 months later, I decided to make the move to the "Land of 10,000 lakes." It was October of 2010. I had just called off my wedding, one that I had spent two years planning with a man I spent over 11 years with. I wanted to be on the ground in Minnesota so I could help Dennis. By this time, we already had a fledgling selection of shirts and hats and were sponsoring kids at competitions all over the world. Most people thought I wanted to move because of the new business, but that was only one small fraction. I was suffocating in Texas. Sure, my folks were there, but I was ready for a new adventure. I wanted time to work on me. I wanted four seasons, trees and some peace for a while. The fact that I only knew one person in Minnesota didn't scare me. The only thing that did scare me was not going.

Shortly before the move, we were contacted by Warner Brothers in California. We had come up with a graphic meme for our company mascot. He was a pretty cool looking cartoon yeti dressed in baggy jeans, a t-shirt, Supras and sported our hat. It must have caught their attention because they wanted this character on a poster for an upcoming movie. They were filming in Chicago, but they wanted local brands from Minnesota to make it feel more like where the movie was based, Minneapolis. The only problem was that they wanted a formal agency ad submitted. We didn't have an official commercial ad billboard, so we had to scramble and ended up working with a fantastic advertising guy based out of Denver. After several weeks of hard work, we landed on three concepts and sent them off to Warner Brothers. A short time later we were notified our ad was selected to be a poster in a mall scene in the movie. It was pretty exciting, and it was giving our brand more credence. We were attending events, sponsoring kids, designing clothes and loving every minute of it.

★   ★   ★

In February 2011, two weeks after I finished grad school, a big moving truck showed up in front of my home. I had just bought my very first home, and my name was the only name on the mortgage. It was all mine! I couldn't have been more excited.

I arrived in Minnesota two weeks later to find my home with 5.5 feet of snow in the front yard. That first week didn't get above negative 10 degrees. Cold was not a good definition coming from 70-degree weather. It was a shock to the body on every level. I didn't own a pair of boots, scarves or even a good pair of gloves. I barely had a coat thick enough to brave freezing weather, let alone sub-zero temperatures. Needless to say, I was ill-prepared.

The first real snow happened a few days after arrival. I was excited to see fresh snow, so of course I ran outside. I felt like a kid; the air felt so fresh and clean. I didn't even have a snow shovel yet! On my way to Home Depot, I got stuck in my driveway. I didn't realize that plows come by at night, so you have to shovel the driveway BEFORE you get into the car. Note to self. I had to dig myself out that first time with a dirt shovel.

I was discovering all kinds of new things. I thought that ice dams had something to do with beavers. When my realtor told me to be careful and watch for ice dams in the wintertime, I was horrified. I couldn't figure out how those damn things got up on the roof. In Texas, we always had lots of possums and raccoons, so it didn't dawn on me she was talking about ice melt off.

Within a couple of weeks, when the dust had settled a little bit, I was still going through boxes here and there. I came across all the frames and albums full of my life with Nick. Everywhere I looked, I was seeing him. In pictures, old dried flowers, little things I had collected over the years. I went around and gathered every single image and all of the photo albums and shoved them in every drawer and closet in the house that was not being used. Out of sight, out of mind. This is how I have always dealt with the majority of problems in my life. I suppose I did it because it was easy. If I needed to stop thinking about something, I would just remove it from view, thinking it would just "go away." I could do that just as easily with people. I would just unfriend them, delete all the contacts and emails, and boom, they were gone. It was never done out of spite or revenge. It was survival. I had to keep moving.

★　　★　　★

The move to Minnesota, at least initially, was exciting. And because the business was growing exponentially, it gave me something to pour my heart into. We had our formal launch party in the summer of 2011 complete with custom invites, a logo ice sculpture, catering, custom flat bill cakes, custom brand lighting, you name it. It was a dream come true and the best night of my life.

However, there was a downside. A terrible one for me. I did a really good job at hiding in our business. I was growing increasingly weary of what these 12 to 22-year-old kids who were buying our product would think if they knew this 30 something, morbidly obese woman was the actual face of the company. As time went on, it tore my soul open because I wanted to go to more events. I wanted to be side-by-side with Dennis on this adventure and be proud of what we had built together, but it was not working. I didn't want anyone to know that I was his partner. I thought that my age and weight would ruin us if the kids found out. So subconsciously, I started to withdraw. I was never going to be able to grow the business the way I wanted if I were afraid every day of someone finding out I was the driver behind it all. It broke me.

Later in 2011, we got a call from a well-known casting director and production manager in Hollywood. We were invited to attend the Kids Choice Awards to represent our brand at the formal after-party celebration. Our brand was to go into the "goodie bags" at the party for all the little superstars from the Awards show. It was a red-carpet invitation that would have meant potential massive growth for our humble little company. Who could turn it down?

I did. Because I was afraid. Knowing that we would be at this kind of event almost blew me into a full-blown panic attack and quite frankly, one from which I couldn't recover. I wouldn't be able to hide, and everyone would find out this massively fat woman was the face of our brand. I couldn't do it. I shut myself off in my home and cried my eyes out because I knew I was going to let Dennis down. I was too self-conscious to make a go of it. I wasn't strong enough.

We eventually stopped doing shows because it meant I had to be present. The more I wanted to hide, the more I started eating and the more depressed I got.

The business folded in early 2012. A wonderful start and promising future, but the owner was too embarrassed of herself. The End....

I started second-guessing my decisions, and as weeks turned into months, the days and nights got lonely. I missed my family terribly. I was heartbroken about the business and all I wanted to do was crawl in a hole and die. Once again, I was ill-prepared for the loneliness I would feel, and I became utterly miserable.

It was winter of 2011, and I had been in Minnesota for almost a year. I thought if I moved someplace new and exciting that life would be better. However, every day I woke up, nothing was feeling better. Nothing had changed. I was morbidly obese, well over 350 pounds, and my head was just a clutter of one bad experience after another screaming around in my brain all day. It was like a bad song that I couldn't get out of my head. I was haunted, I was desperate. I wanted the bad memories to go away, I wanted the fat gone, I didn't want to be embarrassed about myself, I felt like a failure and I didn't know what to do. I was willing to try one last thing. Why hadn't I thought of this sooner?

★　★　★

I sat patiently in my seat as I waited for the court clerk to call my name. I had been sitting there for nearly three hours. When I finally heard my name, all I could think of was, "Yikes, here we go."

"How would you like your name spelled?"

"A-T-H-E-N-A"

"Okay, last name?"

I closed my eyes and said, "Perez. P-E-R-E-Z."

"Athena, what is the reason you are requesting this name change today?"

It was a simple question, however, one I had not thought about. I couldn't think of anything else to say. My name felt like an itchy wool sweater that was a size too small. It was mine, but it never fit right.

"Your honor, I have been a Perez my whole life; I would like to make it official. My dad's last name is Perez, and he's the only dad I have got."

"Since there is no one here to contest, I see no reason this request should not be granted."

CLUNK. The loud noise from the stamp hitting the desk startled me. I wasn't sure if it was the loudness of it or the fact it happened so quickly. I looked up, and the judge was motioning me to come to pick up a piece of paper he handed to the court clerk.

"Congratulations Ms. Perez, you are free to go."

I am free to go? That's it? I strolled up to the bench and retrieved my piece of paper. It was a certified copy of the court request to change my name. This whole process seemed far too simple.

I let out a massive sigh of relief as I hurried to my car with my newly stamped court record and threw myself into the front seat. Tears already rolled down my face before I sat down. It was over! I could put my past behind me once and for all. I knew starting the following day I would be a brand-new woman. I knew it! It had all come down to this one day, and it was finally here. No more tears, no more pain and I would have closure. Something I felt I needed to attack this problematic weight problem.

I woke up the next morning and wandered around the house for a couple of hours, but I still felt like the same woman that walked in the courtroom the previous day. It's not that I thought I would hear trumpets blaring, but I thought for sure that the pain in my heart would disappear overnight. It hadn't.

Here's what happened. I created a whole new mess for myself. Now I had to change my driver's license, my social security card, my checks, put in notification with the post office, notify the credit bureaus and notify all my consumer credit accounts. It took weeks to get everything changed over, and all the while, I thought there would be "healing." It never came.

I was still the same mess I was before. There wasn't much benefit that came from this name- changing exercise.

There was no benefit, but there was a harsh lesson that I was finally able to see, and let me tell you, I didn't acknowledge it easily. It's like discovering a lousy habit you never knew you had. It felt terrible.

I was never an athlete; I never had those kinds of skills. But I had developed an unsavory skill of "running." I had done it my whole life and never acknowledged it until I got to Minnesota.

★   ★   ★

Several years before, in 1995, when I turned 17 and started my senior year in high school, I could think of nothing else but getting the hell out of Washington State. I kept telling myself, "As soon as I get out of here, my life will be better." I was patient because I knew if I held out long enough, graduation day would come, and I could leave. I had applied to 23 schools outside the state of Washington and was accepted at nearly all. The decision to leave Washington was easy. Where to go? I had relatives in Texas. I knew this was my chance to start over. Two weeks after graduation, I was living in South Texas. Free at last and free from every horrible chain I had ever felt. No more heartache, no more bullying, no more haunting memories. It would all be gone, and finally, the life I had waited so patiently for, would come.

This didn't happen. Nothing changed; in fact, it only got worse exponentially. During my stay in Texas, I moved 11 times. 11 new addresses, 11 new phone numbers.

15 years later, yet again, I was sitting in a new home 1200 miles north. I had run again, with the same belief that all I needed was new scenery. Moving to a new place and starting over seemed like the perfect solution every time I did it. Every time I ran, I thought once again, would solve everything.

★   ★   ★

I had new and better reasons for moving halfway across the country this time, but let's face it. The heart of the run was to get away and to leave what was left behind. There was an undeniable pull to be here in Minnesota and one that I couldn't ignore. However, there was also a ridiculous amount of past addresses that I couldn't ignore either. There was a more significant issue, and I knew it.

I hadn't taken into consideration that every time I ran, the problems followed me. This is why I went for the name change. If I suddenly became a new person, the old one wouldn't find me. Sounds like good logic, right?

I didn't know it, but I had developed a problem called "Addiction Geographical." Alcoholics Anonymous refers to this behavior as a "geographical cure," which describes someone that moves from place to place to get a fresh start. They might even do it many times, promising themselves that this time it will be different. I was not an alcoholic, but I had the same type of behaviors. I was supposed to know running away from things my whole life wouldn't solve anything, but I didn't. Furthermore, I was also unaware that all those efforts were fruitless.

All those years of moving, I was always thinking I was tying up loose ends before I had detangled any of them. Moving gave me a simple resolution. I had a new address and new phone number but completely forgot that the emotional ties ran deeper than a new address or new phone number. I was never going to get far enough away to escape the unresolved ache I carried in my heart. Somewhere deep down inside of me, there was a little girl that wanted to BUY my home because it would force me to stay and confront my pain (Priebe, 2016).

My new home was a blessing in disguise. It was a complete miracle how I even qualified on my own. Or was it? It challenged me to stay. Leaving was comfortable, but staying was the challenge. I knew I would have to go back and revisit all the issues I abandoned, but it also forced me to start looking forward and being present in all my new ventures.

# LESSON 1

*By Athena Perez with Jennifer Pendleton*

*"When we don't deal with our trauma and our past, we carry it with us, try and run from it, or both. We haven't made sense of our story, and therefore, our past is still impacting our present in countless invisible ways." -- Psychology Today*

*When we disregard trauma, these emotions become displaced and can manifest in bizarre ways we don't understand. We might be fine for a few weeks and then suddenly explode with rage, or fall into sadness and not fully understand why. We hurt and lash out at those closest to us, and withdraw from those we love or retreat from opportunities meant to bring joy.*

*Don't let times of calm fool you. Feelings that aren't addressed in a healthy way are ticking time bombs waiting to go off. It might feel scary to revisit memories you'd rather bury six feet in the backyard, but you will need to deal with them one way or another.*

CHAPTER 2:

# ASK FOR HELP

Not even the name change helped this time. I isolated myself. I cut myself off from every bit of the life I had lived and every person I knew.

I knew I needed to get my life together, but I thought the name change would lift the sorrow and despair I felt. I thought it would give me a new identity. I didn't have to be the hurting girl anymore — the woman who had fought with herself and others her entire life. This name change was a gateway to a new life.

In the beginning of the story, "The Warrior and the Monk," the young warrior carries a sword and a shield, and he pursues dragons and treasures of the Earth. The more he acquires, pursues and achieves, the greater his sense of purposelessness. That's how I felt. I lacked purpose. Nothing I did gave me fulfillment. The young warrior sought the counsel of an old monk. Unbeknownst to the warrior, he was beginning his journey to find God. I needed to find my monk.

As I had done so many times before, I found myself on my knees praying. I am not sure why. I felt that so many of my prayers had gone unanswered. But I continued. I mostly prayed to find a resolution of my past and help me understand how to correct my weight problem. I didn't know what to do or where to go.

★   ★   ★

I was surfing the internet one night and came across an ad for a life coach named Sarah.

"Do you need help with direction? Do you need help defining yourself to create the life you envision?" the ad asked.

"Yes," I whispered.

I was intrigued.

Sarah would be able to put me on the right path and figure out what was wrong with me. Perfect. This was precisely what I needed: a life coach.

After one session with Sarah, she gave me a diagnosis over the phone. She told me I needed therapy. Specifically, psychotherapy.

A psychologist?

I was mortified.

A few weeks earlier, I was getting a manicure at one of my favorite salons. I watched my nail technician whirl the paintbrush to create perfect white tips on my fingernails when I happened to overhear the conversation of the woman behind me.

"Hi Kim, good to see you today."

"Heeeeeey, Dr. Beth. Come sit, come sit."

"How is work going?"

"Just another day on the funny farm."

"Right. Ha! You must get tired of listening to that stuff all day."

At this point, I couldn't help but be curious about what she did for a living, so I turned around in my chair and asked her. She told me she was a psychologist.

"Ahhhh," I said, as I slowly turned back around with my eyebrows raised.

When Sarah told me that I needed psychotherapy, I instantly remembered the conversation in the nail salon and thought there was something wrong with me. I had always been tough. I didn't need therapy. Treatment means something is broken. It's a sign of weakness. Only crazy people needed therapists. I didn't want to be one of those people lying on a couch in some office, talking to a stranger about my life! "That's them," I thought. "I don't need that shit. I am fine."

What in the hell was Sarah talking about anyway?

Just because I moved a lot didn't mean I had trouble facing my life. Just because I wanted a fresh start didn't mean I had severe issues. After all, everyone has problems. I was a homeowner, I had a master's degree, I owned businesses, I mowed my grass, paid my taxes, paid my bills. I was a productive member of society.

But if I were being honest with myself, life was dreary. The days were blending together. Most days I didn't even take a shower or leave my home. I was depressed and lonely. I watched television and ate. I remember little else. The more weight I gained, the unhappier I became. The more unhappy I became, the more I ate.

Several weeks after getting the diagnosis from my "know-it-all" life coach, I begrudgingly started looking for someone I could talk to. My weight was spiraling out of control. I was well over 400 pounds. I was out of options.

My older brother had already gone through several years of therapy and kept telling me to go. I had resisted. I thought I was above it. I was tough, and I didn't need it. I fought it for weeks, but it was hopeless.

I continued to pray.

"God, please send help. I don't know what to do. I don't know where to go. Help me."

This time, there was no escape. I couldn't run. I was a homeowner. I had a responsibility now. I was going to have to face the storm. It was like a slow-moving tornado that made its way onto my porch and rang the doorbell. It had followed me. I knew what I needed to do, but I was not a fan of the idea. At all.

For several days, I read through countless websites and scrolled through what felt like hundreds of "About Me" pages before I stumbled across my therapist, Jamie. Based on the photo on her website, she looked to be in her late 40s. She had a kind smile. The description on her website stated she helped individuals experiencing a crisis, depression, anxiety and concerns with identity, anger management, grief and loss. She coached them in career and life decisions. I couldn't tell you what, exactly, it was that drew me to her. But it was enough. I made my first appointment for a week later.

★   ★   ★

I approached therapy with skepticism.

I was wondering what miracle this woman would be able to pull out of her hat. Somehow I pictured a nicely appointed office with art, a globe and leather furniture that included one of those couches you could lie on. Maybe I watched too many episodes of "Growing Pains" when I was a kid. The character, Dr. Jason Seaver, a psychiatrist, had a couch just like that in his office.

Jamie had a tiny, humble space. The walls were painted a relaxing steel gray with browns and blues decorating the small sitting room that was adorned with a fountain, a bookshelf filled with self-help books, and essential oils. There was also a table with copious choices of teas and coffees. The aroma was relaxing — probably peppermint or lavender emanating from a small, lighted machine in the corner. Her office did have nice leather furniture but not the kind of couch you lie on and spill your guts while you stare at the ceiling. Instead, it was a massively comfy chair with a red velvet blanket. The kind of chair you could fall asleep in.

I was calm and very much at ease on that first visit. Jamie was soft-spoken, and she had a noticeable boho style that I loved. She had wildly curly hair, and I even noticed the tail end of a tattoo on her forearm. There was something that I liked about her almost immediately.

She began my first visit by explaining what would happen in the first three visits. The purpose would be to gauge where I was in order to give her a high-level understanding of what might be needed going forward. Then she would walk me through her findings and detail a plan for the future. It sounded easy enough.

During those initial three visits, we talked about how I ended up in Minnesota, how I felt on a daily basis and a brief history of my background. I didn't go into too many details as she said we would get to those later.

By the end of the third visit, I was diagnosed with Post-Traumatic Stress Disorder (PTSD). This happens when a person has difficulty recovering after experiencing or witnessing a terrifying event (Mayo Clinic, 2020). The simple fact that I had this diagnosis was traumatic for me. I sat there crying and wiping my face.

"Are you sure I have a problem? I mean, I feel fine!"

"Athena, it's OK. You have done nothing wrong, and there's nothing for you to be ashamed of. We are going to work through this together."

I sat there crying for several minutes before I looked up. Jamie had a look of love and empathy and asked if I was OK. I told her I was fine. I would always been fine.

Deep down, I knew I was broken.

I treated myself poorly. I didn't care enough about myself to even shower regularly. It was odd because I could be filthy and still have pretty nails. I am not sure if I treated others badly at the time, but I had been told I was "cold."

I lacked empathy. I would hear people talk about the death of loved ones and bad things that were happening in their lives, and my first thought would always be "they were weak." I had never lost anyone that close to me. I spent years simply wanting certain people to die. I believe years of working in property management and years of litigation contributed to this. When it came time to pay rent, tenants always had a reason for not paying. There was always a death in the family. After years and years of hearing the same thing, I suppose I became a cynic. I never believed anyone's stories anymore. And even if I did, I didn't care. I routinely evicted people around the holidays without a second thought.

I had little understanding of my own behaviors. I knew I was angry, irritable, depressed and suffered frequent panic attacks. I could become quite angry over almost anything. I was always on edge but keenly aware it was a defense mechanism. The problem was I never knew how to shut it off.

I was a rigid black-and-white thinker when it came to relationships or other people. There were no gray areas.

I wouldn't say I thrived on conflict, but I didn't have a problem with it. I had no hesitation about getting up in someone's face. I was severely protective of my home and my property.

I don't believe for a second that I was intrinsically dark, but I had not known any other life. I felt like a broken coffee mug. No matter how much coffee I put in it, it was always going to leak.

"Where would you like to start, Athena?" Jamie asked.

"I mean, I don't know where to start. How does this usually work?" I replied.

"Tell me about all the things you feel right now," she said.

"I feel stuck," I explained. "I feel like I am destined to be unhappy and fat for the rest of my life."

At this point, I stood up and grabbed my stomach with my hands, sobbing.

"Do you see this?" I asked, nearly yelling. "This is what's wrong, and I don't know how to fix it. I think about it every damn waking minute of my day. I want to cut it off. And if I could, I would. That's what's wrong! I just want to be happy!"

"OK, I think we will start there," Jamie said at the end of the session. "Think of this as the beginning of your journey. Your weight problem isn't food. In order for you to deal with your weight problem, you are going to have to recognize that it's the only tool you had to deal with everything you've been carrying around. You've carried anger, guilt, embarrassment, shame, grief, resentment and fear. You are going to have to make peace with these so that you will be able to find new ways to cope. On the other hand, you have tied happiness with this belief that as soon as you get all the weight off, you will be happy, and I have a feeling this is not what is going to make you happy."

At the time, it seemed insurmountable. The goal was to make peace with all of these issues? How?

★   ★   ★

I suppose you could say my journey started in 2012 with a cup of coffee.

I had just made myself a fresh cup of steamy Joe with a splash of half and half fresh off the Keurig. Jamie led me into her office and sat me into what would become my favorite chair.

She began, "If we're going to get the bottom of unraveling the weight problem, we need to understand how it happened and why it continues to happen. You have focused your life on the weight itself instead of the source. Tell me about anger."

I felt awful sitting in that chair the first time. When I finally agreed to therapy, I didn't rejoice in my own bravery. Instead, I got stuck on one thought: I failed.

I had failed to handle my life on my own. This ferociously independent woman could not pull it together. I failed to just get over it. I failed to keep up the appearance that I had my life together.

I wasn't sure if this was going to work, but I knew these feelings and emotions I had carried with me for so long got in the way of feeling happy, of feeling like I was worth something. I am not sure why I had waited so long, other than I knew I was going to have to relive everything. This was not a pleasant thought.

"The young warrior knew he was in the presence of someone who had acquired great wisdom." —The Warrior and the Monk

I bowed my head, took a sip of coffee, put my head back in the chair and let out a huge sigh. My eyes fixed on the silky see-through curtains hanging in the window.

Why did I have a weight problem? What was going to make me happy? Those were reasonable questions. Food was my best friend, but it had also become the enemy. And the person who I felt was responsible for that was dead. I was never going to get the answers I needed. What possible good was going to come from talking about this? I was reluctant to address what still had me angry after all these years.

# *LESSON 2*

*By Athena Perez with Jennifer Pendleton*

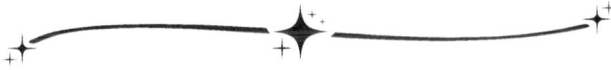

*Asking for help can — and probably will — make you feel vulnerable. Some people equate asking for help with weakness. We risk rejection, and that could mean more devastation.*

*We tell ourselves it's fierce independence, pride or strength, but we all need the help and support of others — even those of us who have had a hard time trusting people in the past. We have to be committed to finding the right person or people to be a part of our tribe.*

*Time is of the essence, too. The longer you wait, the more the emotional gunk will build up. The sooner you ask for help — that could look like finding a trusted counselor or therapist who can help you work through things privately — the sooner you begin to heal.*

*The risk you take by refusing to be vulnerable is cheating yourself of your own fully lived life and potential. Ask for help. It might be the bravest thing you have ever done.*

# CHAPTER 3:
## *THE ROOT*

M y earliest memory in life was one of chaos and confusion.

I was almost 3. It was a mid-May morning in 1980.

I don't remember much of the day other than it went from morning to almost pitch black quickly.

There was a certain hustle and bustle. I had no clue what was going on other than something was not right. I have 10-second clips of that day. I remember watching my family climb on top of our home's roof to watch the sky.

That morning was May 18, 1980, and Mount St. Helens had just erupted. We only lived about 70 "crow miles" away from the mountain. I remember the ash.

No more than a year later, my parents decided to get divorced. Chaos and confusion grew.

My father and mother initially agreed she would get a place of her own but would be back for us when she was settled. For about nine months, it was just my two brothers, my father, Brad and me.

Brad worked as a mechanic at Boeing. He woke up at 5 a.m., drove us to our grandparents' house, then picked us up at night to go home. We spent our days watching "The Price is Right," spending time with our aunt and uncle who were young teenagers at the time, and helping my grandmother deliver newspapers. We would load up her car with bundles of papers, and all three of us kids would ride around in her 1980 blue Chevy Citation all day and take turns sticking our bodies out the window as we stuck rolled up newspapers into plastic mailbox-like holders at the edge of sidewalks.

On the weekends, Brad made us pancakes with chocolate chips, peanut butter and syrup. He even gave the concoction its own nickname: "Gook pancakes."

We belonged to a Mormon church, went steadfastly every Sunday and sang songs like "Choose the Right" in primary.

My parents' divorce was final in the fall of 1981. Shortly thereafter, Brad met a woman named Shelly. She was the same age as Brad and had three small boys the same age as the three of us. We knew them from the church. When they started dating, there was a period of happiness. We were excited at the prospect of getting a new mom, especially since ours wasn't around that much. Shelly lived with her boys at her mother's house a few miles away, and we would call her on the telephone often to say hello. Initially, the three of us kids were so excited about this beautiful new lady in our life.

By July 1982, Brad and Shelly were married. I had just turned 5. On Shelly and Brad's wedding day, Shelly told me I was not allowed to have any of the cake because I was fat. I didn't know what fat meant, but she said it harshly. She told me I needed to lose weight. The average weight for a five-year-old was 39.5 pounds. I was almost 80 pounds.

To her point, I was big for my age. All those months of macaroni and cheese and Gook pancakes added up. I was a bit of a chunky monkey. Even my nickname had changed from "Tini Bean" to "Tini Tank."

The day she and Brad got married, she said, "We're going to fix this real quick." I wasn't clear what that meant, but I was about to find out.

The prospect of this beautiful new mom was short-lived.

During the first few weeks, it was clear who her favorites were. My two brothers and I would be in bed, while her three boys were out in the living room eating snacks and staying up late. When we would stick our heads out our bedroom doors and ask if we could come out too, Shelly would yell at us to get back in bed. And when it came to daily household chores, the three of us carried the bulk of the load. We folded and put away laundry, mowed grass, washed dishes, swept and scrubbed floors, dusted and every other task that meant keeping a clean home. Shelly did the cooking; the kids handled pretty much everything else. I am sure much of this was because she was sick all the time. She had juvenile diabetes and was continually fighting light-headedness, sugar highs, poor circulation in her feet and fatigue.

Within several weeks of her moving into the house, I was forced to get on the bathroom scale for what became a daily "check-in." As long as the same number or something lower showed up, I was fine. If the scale showed I had gained even an ounce, there would be punishment.

As a child, I used to sing a lot. It kept my mind busy during my seemingly endless daily chores. As she watched me scrub floors on my hands and knees, Shelly would walk by me and start singing the song "Work" from Walt Disney's animated movie, "Cinderella." She seemed to get a kick out of calling me "Cinderella." For my fifth birthday, she gave me a copy of the book. On the inside cover, she wrote, "Dearest Athena. I thought you would love this book. You two have so much in common." Shelly would plug her nose with her fingertips and make fun of how I sang. "Athena, you sound like you sing with your nose plugged," she said. "Look at me." Then she would dance around mocking me. I would get embarrassed and stop singing.

Once, Shelly asked me what I wanted to be when I grew up. I told her I wanted to be a singer. Shelly shrieked with laughter just like the wicked stepmother in "Cinderella."

It became clear in short order she had a strong distaste for me. She laughed at me, made fun of me and seemed to get pleasure watching me do manual labor. One morning, after I had just finished cleaning the bathroom, I moved the mop and bucket into the hallway and went to tell Shelly the bathroom was clean. She had a routine inspection. She'd run her finger over the bathroom mirror ledge and behind the faucets to make sure I hadn't missed an inch. This one particular morning I had missed a spot behind the toilet. Keep in mind, I was 5-years-old.

Shelly suddenly shrieked.

"You missed a spot! Look at what you did," she yelled.

The next thing I know, she grabbed my ear with her pointer finger and thumb and threw me to the floor. She shoved my head behind the toilet so I could see the small hair that was left on the floor. She was right: I missed it. I got spanked. Shelly started brutally swatting me so hard I started crying. That only infuriated her further, leading her to hit me harder and longer. The beating continued until I stopped crying. Shelly beat me so much that day that she started breathing heavily. She threw me to the floor inside the bathroom and slammed the door. I don't remember how long I sat there, but I was late for school.

Punishment for missing spots would mean I had to do it all over again. About this time, one of her boys came running down the hallway and knocked over the bucket of water I had just moved into the hall. There was punishment for doing such a silly thing like leaving the bucket of water in the hallway. The wet floor was all my fault. I sat there for six hours the first day and nearly eight hours the second with a hairdryer, drying the floor by hand. I was not allowed to get up until the floor was dry. My lunch was delivered to me while I sat there with this hairdryer in my hand. When I went to turn the hairdryer off so I could eat, she came running over and clocked me against my face with the back of her hand. So, there I sat, waving around this hairdryer, quietly eating my peanut-butter-and-jelly sandwich, and crying.

Yelling and screaming seemed like a daily occurrence. Shelly was always yelling at me for something.

It wasn't just the way she yelled at me; it was shrieking. She literally scared the piss out of me. One morning she was screaming about something, and I felt wet. I looked down. I had peed my pants. This happened all the time. I would get sent home from kindergarten because I was constantly pee-ing my pants; the thought of going home scared me. I was peeing myself almost every day. And Shelly's punishment for such an act was remaining in my soaked clothing. I started getting horrible rashes. The insides of my legs and private parts developed sores. To remedy this, Shelly ordered me to get undressed one morning, grabbed me by my hair and tossed me into the bathtub. She told me to lie down and spread my legs. She then poured rubbing alcohol on my sores. I started screaming. The louder I cried, the more she poured.

"This is what happens when you pee yourself," she yelled.

I cried myself to sleep that night, hoping the burning would stop. I didn't stop peeing my pants until I was almost 8-years-old.

When the punishments became more brutal, Shelly would hit me harder, leaving bruises. If I cried "no," it only made the situation worse.

After crying "no" one morning, Shelly pushed me into the kitchen. She made me stand in front of the pantry while she fumbled around for hot sauce. She forced me to drink it straight out of the bottle. I cried because it felt like my tongue was burning off. Crying was OK. I learned that early on. But I had better not utter a single word. And hot sauce was not her only weapon. She also frequently used a concoction of chili flakes, dish soap and cod-liver oil. She learned that the latter made me vomit, so anytime I was caught with food, I would have to drink it. Cod-liver oil also had side ef-fects, including diarrhea, stomach aches and nosebleeds.

Within the first year of her moving into our home, she made most foods off-limits. I was allowed to have what she put in front of me: very little. Breakfast might be half a grapefruit. Lunch might be a slice of bread with a dash of peanut butter on it. For dinner, I was allowed to have what ev-eryone else was having, but usually much smaller portions — usually about half. I was not allowed any sugar of any kind. If I were caught eating sugar, there would be punishment. Within a year I was down from about 80 to 55 pounds — a perfectly normal, healthy weight for a 6-year-old.

But I was a growing girl, and my portion sizes weren't increasing. I was hungry all the time. It got to the point where I could think of nothing else but food. Yet, Shelly was still calling me "fat" all the time, and food restrictions were still in full force. I would lie awake at night trying to figure out how I could sneak food.

One night, I made my very first daring attempt.

I waited until everyone was asleep and could hear Brad snoring in the bedroom. Shelly slept on the couch and was a light sleeper, so I had to be extra cautious. I opened my door and checked the house — the lights were off, and everyone was sleeping. I got on my hands and knees and crept as softly as I could, making sure I avoided all of the well-known spots in the hallway that could make the slightest creak. I got to the kitchen, and, out of view, quietly opened the bag of soft, white Wonder Bread. I took four slices, shoved them into my nightgown pocket and got back on the floor, making it back to my bedroom undetected. In the dark, I devoured the bread and felt pure joy. At that moment, nothing was more delicious than those slices of Wonder Bread. That's when I started thinking, "OK, don't feed me. I will get the food myself." This was my revenge. I hated Shelly. I was going to find a way to eat whether she approved or not. But, stealing food as a 7-year-old also meant getting caught a lot. I was not exactly a smooth criminal, and my intense hunger led me to act without considering the consequences. And there were always consequences.

After we got home from church one Sunday, Shelly already had lunch on the table. She pointed to one of the head seats. On the table in front of the chair was a massive metal bowl filled with salad and a large pot of soup next to it. She told me to sit, so I did. Then she proceeded to announce to everyone at the table that I was going to eat every bit of that salad and soup. It was enough to feed the entire family.

I tried. But after an hour, I hadn't made a dent. The rest of the family had left the table; I was eating alone. I felt like I was going to pop. I told Shelly I couldn't eat anymore. She responded by shoving my face into soup and salad while she screamed at me to eat it. With food particles on my face, I started again. But, I just couldn't. I told Shelly I was going to throw up. She was unfazed.

The inevitable happened: I vomited into both the salad and the soup. Shelly ordered me to keep eating. So, I did. When Shelly finally realized I was not going to eat anymore, she made me cover the soup and salad with plastic wrap and put them in the fridge. The salad and soup were my meals for the next two days. I was not allowed any other food until the soup and salad were finished — puke and all. It was either that or go hungry. I opted to eat the puke. It could have been worse, I guess. I plugged my nose so I couldn't smell the vomit and took one bite at a time, swallowing without chewing so I wouldn't taste anything.

The only reprieve I had from the hell that was my life was school, church or visiting my mom twice a month when she picked us up for the weekend. When I was in first grade, I spent most school days going through other kids' lunches while they were out on recess. I enjoyed looking at all of the food they got to have for lunch: Ding Dongs, Twinkies, trail mix. I thought I had found heaven. I got caught in the coat closet one day eating another kids' lunch, and I got sent home with a note for Shelly. It was in a sealed white envelope, so I wasn't able to read it. But I knew the teacher was going to tell her what I had done. Within five minutes of handing Shelly the dreaded envelope, she stripped me down and beat me with a wooden stick that she and Brad kept in the kitchen on top of the refrigerator. It was about a foot long, maybe around two inches thick, and it had duct tape wrapped around the end of it — for better gripping, I imagine). Shelly hit me on the backs of my legs, my back and my butt until I had welts on the sides of my legs. I don't believe there was any part of my childhood when I was without bruises on my butt, legs or lower back. Even my hands were scratched and bruised from trying to block the blunt force of these stick beatings.

Getting caught stealing food from other kids' lunches elicited a new punishment Shelly called "prison sentence." It meant bread and water for my meals. That was it. A piece of Wonder Bread with a thin layer of butter and an 8-oz. glass of lukewarm water. I had "prison sentence" for dinner that night and spent the rest of the evening in my room. The next morning, I was introduced to punishment Number Two: "restitution."

"Restitution" was a word Shelly used to describe my payment for sins. If any of us kids got in trouble — primarily me and my older brother Jay — we had to make restitution. This was usually some form of labor. We had to wash walls, weed flower beds, edge the yard with our fingers, cut the grass with scissors, pull weeds from the yard, scrub sidewalks. This was in addition to our already daily chores. Jay and I spent countless days weeding from the time we got home from school till it got dark outside.

I wasn't allowed gloves or a shovel. I had to do yard work with my bare hands, so it wasn't uncommon for me to have bleeding sores near my fingertips. I started biting my nails to avoid the pain of pointy weeds or dirt getting caught beneath my nails. Because Shelly didn't like the fact that I started biting my nails, she punished me for it. Every time she saw me biting my nails, she slapped me. Sometimes across the hands, but many times across the front of my face. Because of this, and the fact that my face wasn't protected while I completed my "restitution" outside in the hot sun, my lips became horribly chapped. That led to me licking my lips, which left a red ring around my lips. To remedy this, Shelly gave me rubbing alcohol. And then there was the duct tape. If she got tired of me licking my lips, she would put duct tape on them so I couldn't lick them. Duct tape was used for other kinds of punishments, too. Sometimes she made me sit at the dinner table and watch the entire family eat while I had duct tape over my mouth. I was so hungry. But I could do nothing more than look down at my lap and let the tears hit my dress.

I earnestly tried to be a good girl. I would do everything Shelly wanted me to do. I would go out of my way to do things for her. Sometimes, those efforts were rewarded. One time, Shelly allowed me to go with a girl from church to gymnastics after school. Within two weeks, I was doing splits and cartwheels, and was getting good and almost completing the no-handed cartwheel. One day after gymnastics, I wanted to show Shelly what I had learned. The coach even had a discussion with her that night about how good I was getting and the fact I might also be a natural! That was the last time I got to go to gymnastics.

Around this time, my right leg started hurting a lot. I was seven at the time, so I dismissed it. It was always a source of discomfort. The right leg itself started bowing outward and it prevented me from doing many of the things that normal kids do, like running and jumping around. I told Shelly about it many times and her response was, "Well good, you shouldn't have been doing gymnastics anyway. Now it won't hurt anymore." I learned that complaining about it was only going to lead to her mocking me, so I stopped telling her about it. She and Brad never took me to the doctor to have it checked out. Later, I often wondered if my leg was a result of Shelly's beatings. At the time, however, I blew it. Whatever it was, I figured, it would heal. Plus, it wouldn't matter because I was never allowed to play any kind of sports anyway.

A short time later, I was offered piano lessons by a lady in the church in exchange for keeping an eye on their daughter while she was giving lessons. At my first piano recital, I successfully played the theme song to "Close Encounters of the Third Kind" — not an easy piece. The claps were huge. I was so proud of myself. I smiled at Shelly and Brad with sheer pride. That was the last time I got to play the piano. I was seven years old.

I started to learn that if I showed strengths or interests in anything, they would be shot down or taken away. When I wasn't doing restitution, there wasn't much to do but play with my Barbies out in the yard or read books in my room. I had about 20 books on my bookshelf and a small trunk of toys that included Barbie dolls, Herself the Elf, Pound Puppies and Paw Paws. Most of the toys I had received for Christmas or as birthday presents were from my extended family or my mother. I don't remember too many times when I wasn't doing some form of "restitution." I was always in trouble. Crying too loud would get me into more trouble. Continuing to cry after being beaten would get me into more trouble. Eating something that was "unsanctioned" would get me in trouble. Getting the mail would get me in trouble if I hadn't asked to go and get it. If I laughed too loud, I would get into trouble. If I opened up my sandwich and decided to eat one slice at a time — to make it seem like I had more food — I got in trouble. If I licked the peanut butter and jelly off the bread, I got in trouble.

I didn't even look forward to holidays as a child because Shelly was constantly threatening to bar us from celebrating them. Once, I was in trouble for something I can't even remember anymore, and Shelly stated there would be no Easter for me. I walked into the living room after church that day, knowing the Easter Bunny didn't leave me anything because I was so terrible. The Easter Bunny did come. But instead of leaving all the same things she left for the boys — Cadbury eggs and jellybeans — I got pencils and little pads of paper. I ended up being forced to use them to write the phrase, "I will not steal food" over and over again.

★   ★   ★

Jamie looked up at me with a puzzled look.

"Athena, did you ever tell anyone? What about your mom?"

"I saw her sometimes, but many times my brothers and I didn't see her for weeks or months."

"Did you ever think about telling your mom?"

"I couldn't," I started.

"Why?"

"John."

"Who was John?"

# LESSON 3

*By Athena Perez with Jaime*

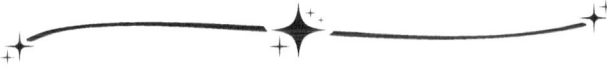

*You cannot change what you don't acknowledge.*

*It's common to devalue our own trauma. We think it will go away with time or that we need to just suck it up and move on. We make comparisons.*

*"Other people have it worse; I shouldn't feel this way. Other people's suffering was way worse than mine." Or, a personal favorite of mine that I heard growing up: "Stop your whining; it could be a lot worse."*

*Unresolved trauma and grief reinforce the idea we are not good enough; we aren't special and we don't have the right to feel what we feel. But all of our trauma and grief are 100% real and 100% felt — and you must honor it.*

*Someone out there has lost their dog. Someone was a victim of crime. Someone was abused as a child. Someone was a lonely latchkey kid. Someone had an alcoholic family member. It doesn't matter what it was.*

*If you deny your trauma, it will lie dormant. And then what happens? You replace it with destructive behavior. And by the time you try to deal with it years later, you'll have forgotten how it all started in the first place.*

# CHAPTER 4:
## *ANGRY*

When my mother left our home, she started dating and eventually married a man named John.

John was a gruff trucker, wore cowboy boots and obnoxious belt buckles, had a gold tooth and reeked of cigarettes and alcohol. I am not quite sure I understood my mother's attraction to this guy, but he was around during our visits. He had a short temper, drank too much and I never felt comfortable around him. He always made me sit on his lap and wanted to touch my arms and legs. I remember my mother yelling at him a few times because of the way he looked at me. I wanted to feel completely safe on my visits to mom's house but never did because of him. He always grabbed us too hard and yelled a little too loudly. John scared me. I never wanted to be left alone with him. Every time I saw him, I felt dread in my gut.

When my mother married John, we didn't see her that often. Most of the time, it was once or twice a month, at best. But there were many months we didn't see her at all. She was on the road doing long haul deliveries across the county, typically food to restaurants, so she wasn't always back in town during scheduled visits. During one of our regular weekend visits, my older brother Jay woke me up in the middle of the night. He was upset and kept repeating, "Athena, we need to call the cops." I woke up quickly. I could hear the screaming and sounds like a rock hitting a wall.

Jay had walked into the living room to find John hitting our mother and tossing her around the room. Jay was terribly afraid but asked what was going on. John yelled at my mother for Jay to get back to bed. Mom crawled over to Jay. Her lip was bloody, and her hands were bleeding. She put her hands on my brother and told him it would be OK, and to go back to bed. Jay now had blood on his pajamas. This was when he came to wake me up.

We sat huddled in my room together crying. We could hear John yelling, my mother screaming and loud clunks and thuds and things breaking. My six-year-old brother Luke was now awake. He was crying and squeezing his teddy bear. The three of us kids got off the floor and headed out to the garage where the sounds were now coming from. The noises, yelling and screaming became louder. We opened the door to the garage. John had my mom up against a wall by her throat, her feet slightly dangling. She was so bloody you could barely see her face. One of her eyes was almost swollen shut, and her lips were the size of baseballs. I peed my pants. "John is going to kill my mother," I thought. There was blood on the wall, blood all over her and John was just wailing on her. Horrified, my brothers and I ran back inside. Jay called the police.

"Please hurry," he yelled. "He's going to kill her. Please hurry."

The three of us kids could do nothing but huddle together and cry while we waited for the police to show up. I don't know how long it was, but pretty soon we could hear sirens in the far distance. All the while, John's out in the garage beating the crap out of our mother.

The police showed up, and we watched as they handcuffed him and put him in the back of the cop car. An ambulance also arrived to treat my badly wounded mother. John was beating his head against the window, spitting on it AND yelling, "I am going to fucking kill you. I am going to fucking kill you." John ended up getting hogtied and tossed into the back of the police car because he wouldn't quit hitting the window with his head.

I wish I could say this was the last time I saw John, but it wasn't.

I was seven years old, and no place felt safe — not with my father, Brad or my mother. Even at that age, I was fully aware that my mother could not save us from our hell. She was having a hard-enough time saving herself.

It was hopeless.

I prayed a lot when I was young. I prayed for the spankings and beatings to stop. I prayed that Shelly could love me. I prayed that she would stop being angry.

I prayed to God. I begged him. He never came.

I was still sneaking food, in fact, more so than ever. I was stealing whatever food I could get my hands on — frozen bread out of the freezer. I was even breaking into people's homes and robbing their refrigerators.

There was an old man and his wife who lived behind us. The back door to their garage faced my family's yard. I would wait until I knew it was his nap time, and then I would sneak into his garage and steal food out of his freezer. One day, I scored the motherload: a frozen loaf of chocolate zucchini bread. All I had to do was wait for it to thaw. I stored my prize in the back of an old truck that sat in our backyard. Brad used it for lawn clippings. I hollowed out a tiny hole in the old smelly grass mound. I didn't care because the loaf of bread was wrapped in tinfoil in a plastic bag. I could come out and take bites anytime I wanted. These moments in my childhood felt like heaven.

One morning, soon after the chocolate zucchini bread discovery, I got on the bathroom scale during our usual morning check-in, and I was up two pounds. Shelly went ballistic. She accused me of sneaking food, which I had, and was yelling at all the boys in the house, "Your sister wants to be fat." She yanked all my clothes off, and I stood there trying to cover my private parts while she continued calling all the boys to come to the bathroom.

"Look at your fat sister! Now, walk by and tell her how fat she is!"

I could tell none of them wanted to do it. But if they didn't, Shelly would have punished them too. One by one, she paraded each boy by the bathroom so they could gawk, make faces and point at the helpless, naked little girl in the bathroom.

Sneaking food and gaining weight on top of that would mean punishment. And punishments were getting increasingly severe. I would receive "prison sentence" in the morning and nothing for the rest of the day. Some days I didn't eat.

There was a time when I was confined to my room for almost 10 days. Shelly didn't allow me to leave. I was so hungry, I felt pain. I was hungry, alone and bored, with no human contact during the day. I could hear the boys coming and going and conversations, but I was not permitted to even open my door. I had to go to the bathroom so badly one day, I couldn't wait to ask Shelly. I ran across the hallway to the toilet and started peeing. She came into the bathroom, ripped me off the toilet as I was peeing, threw me against a wall in my bedroom and told me I was not going to come out of my room. Then she padlocked my door.

Several hours later, nature called again. Desperate that Shelly wasn't answering my calls asking to come out of my room, I had no choice but to climb four feet up to my window, slide it open and hang my butt outside to poop. I wiped my butt with my hand and then wiped my hand on the nearest article of clothing I could find, hoping Shelly wouldn't see it the next time she did laundry.

During that 10-day confinement, I sometimes would preoccupy myself by opening my window to talk to the kids next door. Hearing this, Shelly duct-taped my window shut and covered it in aluminum foil up so I couldn't see outside. Only tiny slivers of daylight made their way through. Shelly turned off my bedroom light and shut the door. I sat there, waiting, thinking, staring at the walls, clutching my blanket. The light from a tiny desk lamp was the only light I had.

After almost 10 days, Shelly allowed me to come out to use the bathroom. I hadn't had a substantial meal in all that time. I was weak, exhausted and all I wanted to do was sleep. I tried to talk to my brothers through the air-conditioning vents in my room but didn't realize how loud I was, so there were occasional spankings.

Once, when I was on the floor playing with my Barbie dolls, she walked in on me, as she often did. The next thing I knew, she was gathering all my toys and throwing them into garbage bags. I never saw them again. She only left the books on the bookshelf. So, I started reading a lot. There was nothing else I could do. I read books and slept. I didn't talk to anyone. I laid in bed and thought. I thought about food. I thought about running away, I thought about grabbing a knife from the kitchen and stabbing her in the throat when she slept. I thought about every way I could hurt her and make her bleed. I was eight years old.

To say that I hated her — not a word I use today — would be an understatement. I loathed her.

Next to my bed was a book in which I kept a stick. I had used a heavy ballpoint pen to chisel the stick into an almost perfect spike. I thought about pulling it out of the book and stabbing her in the side of her throat. I would squeal in excitement; it was only a matter of time before I worked up the courage to do it. The only way to get out my hell was to kill her. So, I thought about killing her almost daily.

After that 10 days, I had had enough. I needed food. I snuck out in the middle of the night. But, as usual, I got caught. This time, I would pay severely.

Shelly ordered me to bring her a tree limb from outside. I brought it to her and she went to town on my butt and the backs of my legs. I wasn't crying very hard because it didn't hurt that much. She got frustrated. She screamed, threw down the limb and got a flyswatter and a bowl of water to dip it in. For those of you who don't know: a wet flyswatter intensifies the snap. She told me to take off all my clothes. I did. I heard the flyswatter whip through the air. It came down and cracked the backs of my knees. It hurt so bad, I instantly screamed. She continued. Whip. Whip. Whip. I was screaming at the top of my lungs. I looked down at the floor to see blood; it was running down my legs. I don't know how many times I got hit, but I couldn't feel the entire backside of my body. A neighbor girl from two blocks away heard me screaming and even came down to see what was going on. When my father got home, Shelly told him how bad I had been, so he stormed into my room with the stick, grabbed my arm and threw me around, thrashing me again with this stick. That night, I slept on the floor of my room.

I woke up in the morning to Shelly opening my door.

"Athena, sweetheart, come and eat breakfast," she said, looking down at me on the floor.

I managed to get up off the floor but instantly felt my whole body buckle from the pain. I limped to the kitchen and she told me to sit down. I tried to sit down on the wooden chair, but I simply couldn't. She set a pillow on the chair and asked if I was more comfortable. I nodded yes, never looking her in the eye. She brought me a massive breakfast with peach cobbler, orange juice and a muffin. It could have fed a king. I ate silently, thinking there was a catch. She kept hugging me and told me we were having a "mommy-daughter day." We went to the movies and she even bought me popcorn. She told me what happened the previous day would never happen again, and I shouldn't tell anyone. I never did tell anyone, and life for the next month or two seemed happy. She dressed my wounds and kept bandages around my legs and was very attentive. She even let me visit Bethany. I thought I had won the lottery. I was usually not allowed to go anywhere and certainly not to anyone's home.

Other than a next-door neighbor, Bethany was the only real friend I remember. We met at school, and she ended up moving in a few houses down the street.

I spent one morning at Bethany's house laughing and playing like a normal girl. At some point, she pulled out her mini oven that made real brownies. I wanted one so bad! We had a great afternoon playing with that thing. When I got home, Shelly noticed some chocolate around my lips. She grabbed my arm, threw me into my room and told me to stay there. She stormed into the kitchen and called Bethany's mom who explained we were making little brownies in the Easy-Bake Oven. Shelly hit the roof. Not only did I get in trouble for eating a brownie, I also lost a friend that day. The only friend I had. I never got to visit Bethany again.

Now the punishment would recommence. After all, I had made a brownie and eaten it without permission.

When Shelly asked me about the brownie, I started to speak. Before I could finish, she hit my mouth with the back of her hand. I could feel my lower lip getting fat.

"How could you abuse my trust, Athena? I let you go over there, and then you completely disobey me!" she screamed.

I felt another blow to my face. Legitimately, I didn't know making a brownie constituted disobedience. That's when Shelly said there would be no food. I tried to explain that I didn't disobey her deliberately. But the more I kept talking, the more I kept getting backhanded. I got a blow to the right side and then a blow to the left. My bottom lip was bleeding. I had a cut on the inside of my cheek. Shelly resolved this with rubbing alcohol. My punishment: prison sentences.

Shelly dragged me across the floor by my hair and yelled at me all the way to my bedroom.

"Every time I give you a chance, you disappoint me. You are nothing but a lying little snitch! You go over to a friend's house so you can sneak food? You don't ever get to do that again!!"

The never-ending vicious cycle I was stuck in continued endlessly. I was always in trouble. As a result, I was always hungry. So, I was always sneaking food. And, I was always getting caught.

Much of my childhood was spent either outside doing restitution or in my room serving one of Shelly's prison sentences. I never experienced summers like the kind kids talk about. The kind when they had fun and played with friends. I was endlessly weeding or sitting by myself in the dirt killing time because there was nothing else to weed. I learned to live in my dreams. I would close my eyes and imagine I was the girl from the "The Secret Garden," or I was dreaming of ways Shelly would die. The latter became a favorite pastime.

If I wasn't getting hit or punished, I was watching or hearing my older brother get hit or punished. My hatred for Shelly was only fueled by Jay's cries. Although Shelly didn't use food as a weapon against him, he would still get hit or backhanded for not folding a fitted sheet correctly.

Shelly was once giving Jay a haircut and didn't like the fact he kept moving his head ever so slightly. So, she kept smacking him upside the head with the back of the brush. Of course, it hurt like hell. Jay started crying. When he started crying, his head started moving. Once again, Shelly didn't like the fact he was moving his head. She went to the fridge to get ice water and returned to dump it on his head.

I also remember the day Shelly gave me a haircut. I was just shy of my eighth birthday. I was in the bathroom watching Shelly comb her hair. Most people thought she was beautiful. I agreed. She reminded me of a geisha. She had skin so light it was almost white, and she had long, black, flowing hair that almost reached her butt. And she had dark-green piercing eyes. I admired her hair. I wanted my hair to be that long, too. I looked up at her and said, "Look! My hair is almost as long as yours!" That was the wrong thing to say.

Shelly grabbed the brush I had in my hand and smacked me upside the head. She told me I didn't brush my hair enough. She started aggressively brushing my hair, pulling so hard it hurt. I was crying. That made her mad. She grabbed my arm and pulled me into the kitchen where she threw me onto a stool. She stormed out of the kitchen. She stormed around a lot — always stomping her feet in some ridiculous rage when she got mad at me. She came back with a pair of scissors. She grabbed random chunks of my hair and started cutting. I could hear her grunting, shrieking and breathing heavily. When it was all said and done, I had short chunks of hair, long chunks of hair, a disastrous mess. Shelly left the room. I sat on the stool, crying. What did I do that was so wrong? Brad ended up taking me down to a local beauty shop to fix the mess Shelly had made so I wouldn't look so much like a boy. I didn't have much hair left.

By the time I was nine, Shelly had resorted to new, creative ways of making me feel worthless. Now she was threatening me with military school. I didn't care anymore. Military school sounded like paradise compared with the hell I lived in. I was starting to get more and more brazen with the things I did, including setting the girl's bathroom on fire at school when I was in fourth grade. To this day, they never knew who did it. Well, it was me. I was hoping I might die in that trash-can fire. But the blaze quickly extinguished as did my hope of going down in flames.

I also tried running away. On several occasions I made it over a mile away before hanging my head and walking back home. Where was I going? I was more fearful of the punishment I would endure for getting caught. So, back home I would go. I had to think of something else to do, so I started robbing the convenience store a block away. I didn't want money. I wanted food. I wanted candy. I wanted whatever would fit in my pockets. I was numb by this point — numb in my heart. The belief that Shelly and Brad would send me to military school was waning; if they were going to do it, they would have done it already. I had one mission: food. Houses, stores, it didn't matter. If something was within grabbing distance, I was going to steal it.

I was 10 years old and in fifth grade when I got caught with bulging pockets. It was clear I had been at the convenience store. One of Shelly's boys had seen me on the way to school and started running home to tell her. I was not going to go home. I could kill time at school before I would have to face the she-devil. I walked extra slow on the way home and came up to the house. I stopped. All of my belongings were in the front yard. Shelly met me on the front lawn.

"You are no longer a member of this family. You are not going to disrupt this family anymore, Athena. You got your wish. You can leave now," she proclaimed.

She walked back into the house and locked the front door. I sat on the front porch for 14 hours through a frigid night. The next morning, my grandmother — Brad's mother — came to pick me up. There were no goodbyes, and the boys were not allowed to talk to me. I stared out the window in my grandmother's car until I couldn't see the house anymore.

Life was better, I must admit, but I was still scared. They were decent grandparents, but my grandpa was just as physical as Shelly and Brad. I was homeschooled for the remainder of fifth grade, and once a week Brad would drive the 20 miles to drop off my homework. I was not allowed to go back and see my brothers, and I was not allowed to go back to the house for any reason. My brothers did come to see me, but they were only allowed small talk. They were not allowed to "talk about the sister that was no longer a part of the family."

At 10 years old, I was officially shunned from the only home I knew. I was gaining weight. Rapidly. My eating wasn't monitored anymore. There was no lock on the pantry like before. I was still waking up in the middle of the night and sneaking into the kitchen. That habit was clearly cemented, whether I realized it or not.

Five months later, I moved in with my mom.

★　★　★

It took more than six months of twice-weekly therapy sessions before I got through the first 10 years of my life. I was so angry I couldn't articulate my hatred and resentment.

I was pissed off at church members for being so silent when they knew things weren't right.

I was upset with school teachers. How many times did they need to see a kid with a fat lip and bruises before someone called Child Protective Services?

My father never noticed there was anything wrong?

I wanted to hit people; I wanted to throw things. I cursed God. How could he watch a child of his go through something like this? Why had it gone on for SO DAMN LONG!

After several weeks of venting, Jamie looked at me one day and said, "Who are you Athena? What are some of your 'I am' statements?"

I wasn't sure I knew what this meant.

Early childhood — spanning up to 10 years of age — is critical for cognitive, social, emotional and physical development according to UNICEF. Between the age of one and 10 is when a child becomes the person they are going to be. "It is when they learn appropriate behavior, boundaries, empathy and many other critical social skills that will remain with them for life."

Who was I, exactly?

By the time I was 11 years old, I had grown into a terrified girl. I had been abused severely for almost seven years. I didn't have a healthy relationship with food or other people. I had learned that the ones who said they loved you the most were the same ones who hurt you the worst. Because I was not allowed friends, I didn't learn how to be a friend. I learned that hitting, screaming, crying and pain was normal. I learned that the desire to inflict pain and suffering on another human was a normal feeling. I learned that the feeling of wanting to kill someone was a normal feeling. I learned that I was fat, I was unwanted, I was ashamed, I was embarrassed, I was self-conscious, I was not capable of skill or talent. I felt like I was nothing more than an unwanted dog, kicked out of the house to lie in the rain and cold.

I didn't know who I was. I only knew what I felt, and it was awful.

"I am stuck," I told Jamie.

# LESSON 4

*By Athena Perez with Al Sagapolutele*

*Anger has trigger points.*

*Anger is different for each of us and experienced in different ways. For some, anger is apparent. We get visibly upset, we yell, scream and/or throw things. Worse, anger can lead some people to cause physical harm to others.*

*Some of us internalize anger. We still feel the internal rage; we just do an excellent job of hiding it. But it tends to manifest in other ways, like addiction to food or alcohol. When internalized anger is not addressed, it leads to self-destructive behaviors. Bottled-up emotions are similar to a pressure cooker. Eventually, the steam will find an outlet.*

*Anger holds us back. We can't move forward when we're always mad. Anger is a distraction. We're rarely angry about what we're ranting about; it's a coping mechanism for dealing with the real root of an issue.*

*Anger can also be a defense mechanism. We feel it when we've been wronged, and the wrong was never righted. So, we carry that wrong with us for so long that eventually, you no longer recognize it. Some of us eat, others drink ourselves into stupidness or maybe both. It's called coping (or self-medicating). It keeps people at bay. You can't hurt me if I hurt you first.*

# CHAPTER 5:
## *GUILT*

I had dreams when I was young that when the abuse stopped, life would be perfect. But it was far from it.

Instead of enduring physical abuse, I carried incredible guilt over something I felt was entirely my fault.

When I moved in with my mom, she had remarried to a man named Chris. He seemed to be a wonderful guy, and it appeared that he treated my mom well. He was very kind, and I felt safe around him. However, it was made clear to me he wasn't entirely comfortable with me moving in.

Life, for the most part, was good for a while. Chris was gone quite a bit because he was also a long-haul trucker, so it was frequently just my mom and me. She had quit driving trucks by this time, and was bartending and cleaning apartments. I used to love going with her to clean apartments because I was making a dollar an hour helping her clean; I thought I was rich. The first thing I was ever able to buy for myself was a Debbie Gibson "Out of the Blue" cassette tape. I mean, seriously, could life get any better?

Twice a month, my mother and I would drive an hour to pick up my two brothers Jay and Luke. I was so excited every time I got to spend time with them. I missed them terribly. Some of my only fond childhood memories were of these weekend visits with my brothers. We always had such a great time together. We mostly hung out, but watched a lot of movies. "Short Circuit," "Commando" and "The Neverending Story" were our favorites. I have seen all three probably over 100 times.

Besides those weekends, I spent my time alone. I felt as if I had been in prison for the first 10 years of my life, so the first thing I did was cling to what gave me comfort: food.

Food became my best friend. It was never going to hit me, speak ill of me, make me feel bad. On the contrary, it made me feel great.

I was gaining weight at incredible speed.

I would wake up around 6 a.m. My mother had already left for work, so I was left to my own devices. I would make heaping bowls of Malt-O-Meal with a half-a-pound of butter and scoops and scoops of white table sugar. It was heaven. If that weren't enough, I would make a pan of brownies and eat until I felt like I was going to throw up. Then, I would throw the rest in a bag so I could devour them at school. When I got home from school, eating was the first thing I did. It might have been downing an entire box of macaroni and cheese, grilled cheese sandwiches, ice cream, tubs of potato salad. It really didn't matter what it was. I could make a massive meal with just about anything. Many times, it was merely working myself through cans of vegetables until I got too full to eat. I wouldn't even warm up the food. I would open the can and eat right out of it. Even today, I still eat vegetables right out of the can. Even more comical, peanut butter and jelly sandwiches are still my go-to when I am upset.

I was 11. There was no rational thought about eating good or bad. There was no thought about gaining weight, what the consequences of eating anything and everything might be down the road. I just couldn't stop. I didn't want to do anything but sit at home by myself and eat.

When I wasn't eating, I was hiding stockpiles of food in my room — in drawers, under my bed, in my closet. There was no conscious thought about why I did it, I just did. From time to time, my mom would come across my hidden stashes.

"Athena, why are you hiding things in your room? You don't have to do that anymore. You know this, don't you?"

I would always nod yes. But, truth be told, I didn't even know I was doing it. It made me feel terrible because I just don't remember even doing it. I couldn't explain how anything got there.

My classmates didn't understand why I was the heavy one. There was no attempt to understand. Instead, kids made fun of me because I was different. I was quiet, I was big, and I didn't look like them. Outside the protection of class, I was on my own. The school bus became a daily torture chamber. Nobody wanted me to sit next to them and made it obvious if I had to sit down next to one of them. I rode to school hearing kids making pig and "oink" sounds.

Many times, I would get to school and find gum wads in my hair that I would spend the rest of the school day picking out. I didn't partake in recess. I didn't want to subject myself to even more verbal abuse. I usually stayed inside at my desk, quietly waiting for the recess bell.

I desperately wanted to feel accepted. I just wanted the other kids to stop teasing me. So, one year at Halloween, I decided to ask my mom if I could throw a party. I was excited when she said "yes" because it was the first time I had done anything like that. The idea I could have a party had me elated. Wow, a real party.

I spent time with my mom carefully crafting cute little invitations and gave them to my entire sixth-grade class. I got home from school on the night of my Halloween party, and my mom had the whole house decorated — orange-and-black crepe paper strung from one end of the house to the other, balloons, Halloween decorations and an entire table full of Halloween treats. The place looked amazing. Not only that, my mom was all dressed up like a devil. I squealed with excitement!

I hurried to get ready so I could start greeting my classmates when they arrived. As it drew near the party start time, one friend had shown up. I was getting worried because no one else had come. The two of us sat there and eventually were joined by the next-door neighbor girl. I wouldn't exactly call her one of my closest friends. However, it did add a body in the room.

Nobody else showed up that night. I tried to hold back tears several times, but the three of us did our best to enjoy our night and eventually left our party to go out and do some trick-or-treating. Trick-or-treating was also something that was a new activity. I had been allowed to go when I was younger, but I had never been able to keep my loot. This time I would be able to not only keep the bag but eat every single piece.

When I got home that night, I broke down in my living room. I felt terrible for my mom who had spent a great deal of time putting together such a lovely looking party for me. In fact, I felt awful. The terrible feeling I had quickly turned to anger. Why were they so mean to me? Distrust of other kids started here. I was perfectly fine at this point keeping my friend circle tiny. Who needed the rest of them anyway?

★   ★   ★

Toward the end of fall 1988, I could feel the tension in my new home.

I loved living with mom, and I adored Chris, but they were starting to fight a lot. Most of the time it was behind closed doors. So, in most cases, I didn't know what, exactly, the arguments were about. I knew I was the topic of a few discussions. Chris was a bit of a neat freak, almost to the point of having obsessive-compulsive disorder. Everything had a perfect place, and nothing should be out of order. I was a kid, so frequently I left messes. It was clear this bothered him a lot. My mom and Chris were also having frequent discussions about my mother applying for permanent custody. I think a part of Chris believed this new living arrangement was going to be temporary, so my mom talking "permanent" was a struggle for him.

Around that time, my mom quit cleaning houses and took a job driving a school bus. I started meeting many of the people she worked with including a guy named Tony.

One night I woke up in the middle of the night to hear yelling and screaming. I crept to the door of my mom's room and knocked on it. I asked if everything was OK. I could hear her crying, and she told me she was fine and to go back to bed. I got home from school the next day, and she sat me down to tell me that she and I were moving out.

What?

She and Chris were going to get a divorce.

The reasoning?

My mom said Chris didn't want children. He was fine with me visiting, but did not want me living with them permanently. Chris gave my mom an ultimatum: "Either she goes, or I go."

I can't tell you how heartbroken I felt. I was happy that I was going to be living with my mom permanently, but feeling like it was my fault was something I just couldn't process. The fact that I was getting ripped out of somewhere I felt safe was devastating. Chris wasn't going to be the father figure I had hoped for, and I was angry he would give my mom such an ultimatum.

I remember getting on my knees the night before we left our home. I was bawling my eyes out. The safety I felt was quickly obliterated. I felt so lost. I remember praying for a dad. I thought Chris was going to be that dad, and I was angry at God for taking him away from me.

"How can you do this, God? What did I do? Why, why, why, why?"

I had a father, but he hadn't spoken a word to me since the day I left. Oh, there were a few pleasantries like "hello and bye," but most of the time he made a point of not being around when we went to pick up my two brothers. I don't know if I believed it at the time, but I felt there was still hope he could be the dad I desperately needed him to be. Perhaps me not living with him and Shelly anymore could mean that things would be better, I remember thinking. They would be different. At least this is what I prayed for that night. I just wanted to have a relationship with him. God never answered me.

We left our spacious home and moved into a cramped duplex. I was a little angry. And to think that all of this happened because of me. It was my fault. The guilt weighed a ton. I wasn't even 12-years-old and had to bear the weight on my shoulders that I was the one who caused their divorce — not to mention the weight was rapidly accumulating on my same frame.

My mom and I settled into the tiny duplex and made it our home. Mom started spending more time with these fun new people at her work. I didn't mind because they were great people. One of them, in particular, was Tony. He was quiet but funny and silly. He was the guy that dressed up like a Ninja Turtle for Halloween and pulled stupid pranks with water guns. I enjoyed being around him very much. He and my mom became fast friends as he was also going through a divorce of his own. In May, my mother told me she had a date that week, and I was surprised to hear that it was Tony. It's not that I didn't think he was nice, but he wasn't exactly the guy I pictured my mom dating. I wasn't upset about the date because I liked Tony very much, but I was skeptical. "Here we go again," I thought. As much as I liked the man, I can't say for sure I was ready for my mom to be dating already.

My initial reservation was quickly squashed when I realized what a good man he was. He loved his kids and treated us the same — no better, no worse. He was also a school bus driver after retiring from a 23-year career in the U.S. Army. Within several months, he and my mom decided to move in together.

★   ★   ★

It was late spring 1990 when the phone rang on a late afternoon. It was my older brother Jay. He sounded panicked.

"Bean, get mom right now."

Mom only spoke to him for what felt like maybe a minute or two. She got off the phone and told Tony and me that she had to go pick him up and out the door she went. I didn't know what was going on, but I knew it couldn't be good.

Jay and I had been in the same grade together since kindergarten except that he was a year older. Shortly before his 14th birthday in April 1990, when he was in the seventh grade, Jay had come home from school, and everything he owned was out on the lawn. I suppose now it was his turn. It happened exactly the same way it had happened to me — with one important difference: The school counselor at Jay's school finally tipped off Child Protective Services.

A part of me had really hoped that when I left home things would be fine. After all, I was the one who was the prime subject of Shelly's wrath. The boys had never mentioned there were many problems after I left other than Shelly was her usual bitchy self. Jay was getting extreme restitution times and overextended groundings, but nothing that would make mom or myself worried for his safety. One day Shelly snapped again. I wasn't there to torment anymore, so she turned her lashings to Jay.

A very bitter battle would ensue; my mom was fighting for custody of me and Jay with the potential of including my younger brother Luke. But Luke opted to stay with Brad. Consequently, we were completely cut off from Luke for the next couple of years. It was devastating. We had to testify countless times to the courts about the previous abuse. We were asked if we wanted to press charges, but we opted out since we were safe with our mother. I kicked myself for years afterward for not pressing charges. I would have loved nothing more than to see Shelly and Brad rotting in a jail cell for what they had done, but the possibility there could be peace stopped us from doing it. All we wanted was to live with our mom and get to see Luke.

Losing our little brother was like getting our hearts cut out. I cried a lot. That meant I was milking my frustration and anger and growing bitterness with food. Shelly would send nastygrams to "leave their family alone" when we'd try to send Luke letters. They changed their phone number and started sending our letters back. Luke had been allowed to stay with Brad because he had testified via a guardian ad litem that he'd never been hit. It was true. Luke had never been touched. But we worried about him based on Shelly's previous behavior. Still, there was nothing we could do other than to let time do its thing. Either Brad and Shelly would mess up, or Luke would be old enough to contact us on his own. So, we waited.

When Jay moved in with us, it felt like we were a family. I am not going to say it was easy, especially in the beginning, because Jay was "difficult" with Tony. It's not hard to understand where the anger and distrust came from. Jay had constant lash-outs at Tony, but Tony remained patient. I watched him boil over at Jay quite a few times, but it was warranted.

Aside from the court battle we were going through and the stress that brought, life seemed to normalize. Jay and I started eighth grade together that fall. Now I had a bodyguard. Those same tormentors quickly learned that picking on me and teasing me wasn't acceptable.

School let out one day, and I was waiting on the bus for Jay. But he never got on the bus. I wouldn't say I was worried because he was 14 and did his thing, but I was curious about where he was. I got home, and he and my mother were in the living room. That morning on the bus a kid was picking on me as usual. I guess it happened so frequently that I just tried to ignore it. To me, it was just another day. Unbeknownst to me, Jay had confronted the kid once we got off the bus in front of the school. They got into a fistfight and Jay won. As a result — and because it happened on school property — Jay was suspended from school.

Mom and Tony weren't exactly happy he was suspended, but he didn't get in trouble because he was defending my honor and the other kid threw the first punch. I sat in my room that night almost in evil glee because nobody was going to mess with me going forward. I now had someone willing to beat the shit out of anyone that said mean things. How awesome was this?

Kids always muttered mean things, but I never got picked on by that kid again. Kids stayed away from me, for the most part. As they say, word travels fast in school. Jay became not only my protector, but my very best friend.

During this same time, things took a bit of a surprise turn. Chris showed up at our home one day and started calling my mom frequently. He told my mom how sorry he was and that he wanted her back. I didn't want to have anything to do with Chris. I just wanted him to stay gone.

Thankfully, this was short-lived, and mom realized she was still in love with Tony and had already moved on. But a night or two after Christmas, she got a call and rushed to the hospital. Chris had driven himself out to the mountains and shot himself in the head with a shotgun. A hunter had found him. His heart was still beating, and he was taken to a hospital, but he ended up passing away a day or two later.

It's hard to describe how I was feeling at this point. I thought it was tragic that Chris committed suicide, but here I was struggling with the fact that he and my mom's relationship failed because of me. It was all my fault. Had I not come to live with them, they would have been happy, and none of this would have happened. At least that is how a 13-year-old rationalized it. It was painful watching this, but more so, seeing my mom hurting. I internalized it in the form of food.

By this time, I was 13 and already weighed over 260 lbs. The eating never slowed.

★   ★   ★

Chris's suicide haunted me for years. Yes, I can look back on my childhood now as an adult and say more things were probably going on in the marriage that I wasn't privy to. But my reality was only as I knew it. Chris gave her an ultimatum because of me, he was distraught she chose me instead of him, and he killed himself.

This was a massive burden for a child to carry. Even if it wasn't mine to bear, unfortunately, I did. It was another adult and someone I respected saying, "I don't want you." Yet again, I was always wondering what I had done that was so terrible.

Attacking feelings of guilt were complicated. I obviously had no part in Chris' decision to kill himself. Yet, I internalized this guilt at a young age. It wasn't rational, but there it was.

Letting go of my own judgment was difficult. It required repetition of a mantra in a big way.

Day after day, I had to repeat, "I set myself free from my own judgment," and "I allow myself to live my life knowing I had nothing to do with the decisions of others." Both of these mantras are from, *"Live Purposefully Now,"* by Elle Sommer.

# LESSON 5

*Guilt is the ultimate form of self-betrayal. Although it's a natural feeling, it's not healthy or productive.*

*We often hear how important it is to forgive others, but what about ourselves? Guilt can be an unrelenting source of pain because it simmers, oftentimes subconsciously. It can be terribly infectious and self-destructive, and it traps us in a pattern of self-punishment.*

*Guilt keeps us from moving forward, and lack of forward motion creates an enormous sense of burden. Each day you wake up and you need validation of your worth.*

*When we blame ourselves for the bad things that happen to us, we invoke myriad other negative emotions: shame, resentment, anger (at ourselves and others). Self-blame can also become a self-fulfilling prophecy. We are in control of our thoughts and feelings, and if they are overwhelmingly negative or destructive, negativity and destruction is what will manifest.*

# CHAPTER 6:
## *CHILDLIKE*

In order to start making changes, I needed to feel better.

It seemed rather impossible coming from the place I was in. I had managed to talk about my childhood traumas in therapy, but It wasn't like I felt better. I will admit it felt great to get them out in the open. But after more than a year in therapy, there was no light at the end of the tunnel that was going to convince me that one day life would feel very different.

On Jamie's advice, I needed to start doing things that made me feel child-like.

When she first suggested this, I had no clue what this meant. I wouldn't say I had a normal childhood. I never did childlike things.

I was sitting in my favorite living room chair one day, casually rocking back and forth.

"Find things that make you feel like a child," I repeatedly thought.

What was I supposed to do? Go to Walmart and buy a pack of play dough? I was a grown woman. I loved to sew when I was in high school, so that's where I gravitated first.

I started making little sweaters and dresses for my dogs. What a blast I had cutting out these little outfits and taking pictures of my dogs in their new pajamas. It was fun but rather short-lived. I grew bored easily.

I started playing a lot of board games, card games, and then eventually gravitated to an Xbox. When I went to the store to buy my first Xbox, the kid at the counter asked if it was for my kid. I laughed.

"Nope, I am the kid. It's for me."

"Haa! So cool, are you a gamer?"

"What's a gamer?"

He just stood there staring at me looking confused. I gathered it was a term I should have known, but I didn't.

I spent hours and hours learning all these fun Xbox games. Over several months, I amassed quite the collection of car racing, snowboarding, skateboarding, trivia-style and classic arcade games. I would be up past midnight, drinking sodas, eating popcorn and playing these silly games. I had never had so much fun. But this got old, too, when I realized I had a hard time shutting it off and the adultlike Athena still had to work in the morning.

I colored in grown-up coloring books with a new set of markers, watched endless amounts of cartoons, experimented with all different types of crafts, bought myself a bicycle, made picnic baskets and took my dogs to parks.

One weekend, I created a tradition that brought more joy than you could imagine. I now call it "Adventure Saturdays." Dennis, my business partner in Minnesota, who had now become my closest friend, and I would pack up for an adventure. Every Saturday it was something different.

One weekend we drove down to Wabasha, Minnesota, just because it was mentioned in one of my favorite movies, "Grumpy Old Men." Imagine our surprise when we arrived that day to discover the "Grumpy Old Men Festival" was happening that weekend! I judged 13 types of chili, watched people jump off boat docks into icy cold water for a polar bear swim, and played checkers at a local bar.

One weekend it was the Minnesota Zoo, another weekend was a trip down to the southern border just to buy sundries at local Amish artisan stores. There were visits to apple orchards, pumpkin patches, and just driving to random towns simply because we'd never been there. Adventure Saturdays became one of my favorite things in the world.

★    ★    ★

Some of my favorite music is 80s, and, in a weird sort of way, 80s music had become a therapy of its own. Nothing could get me dancing and laughing more than Michael Jackson, Madonna, Debbie Gibson and Lionel Richie. Oh yes, and MC Hammer. Have you ever seen the full 14-minute *"2 Legit to Quit"* video? That would get you laughing too.

It was during one of these nights when I was singing and dancing in my living room that something magical happened.

You see, the only real memories I had before the age of 10 were not good ones. When my brain tried to shut out the bad stuff, it shut out the good stuff too. The first decade of my life felt locked up. And it was — quite literally in many ways.

The very first time it happened I was dancing around, doing my usual thing, and suddenly this song came on called "Strut" by Sheena Easton. I froze in my tracks because something felt familiar. My head was still bobbing back and forth but my eyes kept scanning the room in the most unusual way. All of a sudden I could see this girl in my mind, dressed in very 80s clothing. She was walking down this street with a boombox on her shoulders, snapping the fingers on her free hand and walking like she owned the block. "Strut" was playing loudly on the boombox she was holding. That was Karen. I walked home from school with her one day. I was thrilled to have a memory that wasn't terrible.

I immediately ran to my laptop and searched for the year the song was released. It was 1984. I did the math. I would've been seven or eight. I had a memory. I wondered if it would work again.

About an hour later, it did.

It was about 20 seconds into a song, and I knew exactly what it was. It took me back almost instantly. I saw myself in third or fourth grade. I was curled up in bed under the covers. The only light in the room was the tiny bit of green glow from the big numbers on the pink clock radio I was holding in my hand up near my ear. I had the music on so low I could barely hear it, but it was just enough to wave my arms and legs around in a silent dance while I smiled and lip-synced the song. It was daring and bold. I could have been punished severely for being up so late, and I could have risked getting that little clock radio taken away from me. But I stayed up late so I could hear my song! Survivor's "Is This Love."

I was laughing but mad at the memory at the same time. All this little girl wanted was to be a kid. She wasn't doing anything that warranted a beating. She just wanted to hear a song. She was eight.

★   ★   ★

I took the time to bake, make snow angels and enjoy cups of cocoa with marshmallows. Nothing was off-limits! I was learning to laugh again, I was smiling more. If nothing else was accomplished, I did notice that my smile had a rosy glow that I don't think I had ever known.

Feeling better also meant investing more time in my body — something I never did. I didn't know where to start. There were lingering questions, some from long ago.

Why did I gain weight so quickly? Why did my knee hurt so bad? Was I diabetic and didn't know it? Did I have food allergies I didn't know about?

I never went to the doctor much — only if I thought I was dying. Now, I wanted to know everything.

I made appointments to get my eyes checked and found out I needed reading glasses. I had blood tests done and found out I had a multitude of allergies from dairy and sugar to evergreen trees. I also was diagnosed with hypothyroidism.

I had sleep studies and found out that I had severe sleep apnea with borderline narcolepsy. That explained my excessive daytime sleepiness. I met with a heart specialist after learning Brad had a heart condition. My heart was tested, and the tests came back routine with nothing to worry about.

I found a local dentist to make sure my teeth were being cleaned regularly.

I found a good women's doctor to run every test known to man to find out if my feminine parts were fine and if I were able to have children. I tested positive for polycystic ovary syndrome but was physically able to have children.

I even started seeing an orthopedic doctor after I requested X-rays on my right leg. It was time to find out why this leg had been hurting. Finally, in my mid-30s, that right leg had a formal diagnosis: Blount's disease, a growth disorder of the shin bone that causes the lower leg to angle inward. My right knee had collapsed. It is unknown how long I had this problem because the leg started bowing when I was just a child. Most of the time, a diagnosis such as this happens during childhood. Many times, a child can be put in a brace and eventually it straightens out the leg.

Initially, I didn't take the news well. Shelly never believed there was a problem, so she never took me to get it checked out. Nick, my former fiancé, never believed me and was excessively hard on me for not being able to run. I thought I was just weak. But I wasn't weak, and there was a reason it hurt. How in the hell did this not get diagnosed when I was a child?! I was pissed. I was told that it was only a matter of time before I would need knee replacements.

As a result of all these tests, I got reading glasses, a fancy sleep machine to wear at night, took pills for my thyroid and started cortisone shots for my knees. Other than that, I was in relatively decent health.

I say decent health, but what I mean by that is I wasn't going to die. However, that's not to say I couldn't have had a massive heart attack with all the new weight I was carrying. At five feet, five inches tall, I was over 400 lbs. Getting around was starting to get very difficult. I was sleeping better with the new machine, but my mobility was decreasing. My orthopedic surgeon was the one who suggested bariatric surgery.

"Athena, I am a little worried about your legs. If this keeps up, you could lose your ability to walk. You really need to think about getting some pressure off these legs. I am serious."

I heard him. It's not like I wasn't hearing him. I was serious about my desire to lose weight, but I couldn't figure out why I just couldn't make it happen on my own. I would try for a day or two and then give up. One time I lasted 28 days on a juice fast and did very well, but within weeks I was right back to the same way I had been eating before.

His comments scared me, but I dismissed them. I despised the idea of bariatric surgery and wasn't ready for diet and exercise. Exercise, itself, scared me because the condition of my knees and legs was deteriorating quickly.

I wasn't sure what I could do on my legs, but I knew the pool was a place that might be good for them. It would keep pressure off them and just maybe I could burn some calories. Finding a swimsuit wasn't easy, but I found one with a skirt that hid a little of my belly and butt. I signed up at a local, expensive, fancy gym and bought a gym bag. I was ready!

On my first day there, I had just exited the dressing room and was walking to the pool area where two very nice muscular looking guys probably in their mid-20s walked past me. I heard one of them say, "Holy shit, I don't think that pool is going to help much." I tried to shrug it off. It wasn't the first time I had heard something like this. After about an hour in the pool, I looked like a wrinkled Medjool date, so it was time to get out. But there was a group of women in the hot tub that kept looking back at me, whispering and laughing.

"Oh my Gosh, are they waiting for me to get out so they can watch me struggle trying to get up the stairs?" I thought.

They clearly found something funny. I was the only one around, so I assumed they were laughing at me. It was an easy assumption to make.

Instead of getting out of the pool, I was petrified. I ended up staying in there for two and a half hours, waiting for the pool area to be empty so no one could watch when I got out. I never went back to that gym. In fact, I was perfectly fine never walking into another gym again.

A short time later, I stumbled across a cute book about goals on Amazon. It was called My Shining Year. I loved the idea of working on goals. I had never worked on my goals before. I filled the whole thing out and tossed it into a book bin in my living room. I thought it was fun, but I wasn't sure what to do with it. What do you do when we set goals? You declare them and forget about them. At least, that's what I thought.

Buying this first goal book seemed silly at the time. Later, it would become a big deal.

# LESSON 6

*Curiosity softens us.*

*"Growth takes curiosity, curiosity takes courage, and courage requires us to be vulnerable" -- Zachariah Thompson*

*Curiosity also keeps the mind active and opens it up to new ideas and unlocks the door to new opportunities and joy.*

*How do you develop curiosity? You need to be open-minded. You must be willing to learn or unlearn or perhaps even relearn ideas. If you just accept your life as it is without being willing to dig deeper, you will never be able to get below the surface. You must be willing to ask a lot of questions and not be afraid of whatever answers you might discover. "When curiosity is alive, we are attracted to many things; we discover many worlds."*
*--Eric Booth*

# CHAPTER 7:
# EMBARRASSMENT

**"**Athena, how do you feel about your dad now?" Jamie asked.

"Which one are you talking about? My father or my dad?"

"Brad is your father?" she asked.

"Yes."

"Who is your dad?"

I leaned back and smiled. It was probably the first time I had smiled since therapy had begun.

★   ★   ★

Shortly after Chris passed away, mom and Tony's relationship resumed. It wasn't perfect because learning to trust an adult, especially a father figure, was difficult for both me and Jay. Tony and Jay's relationship, particularly during those early months and years, was tough. It was even volatile at times. But as time went on, we came to trust and love Tony.

I started calling Tony "dad" when I was about 13. The day I asked him if I could I was a bit nervous. It came sounding like, "Tony, can I call you 'dad'?" I remember he smiled and chuckled a bit and nodded his head. He felt like a dad to me — perhaps more than Brad ever did. He was very involved in our lives, and we constantly did things together as a family. He was an active parent, and I believe that's what made the difference. In June 1991, Tony and my mom were married, and his relationship as my "dad" was solidified permanently.

This man became someone I loved, cherished, admired, respected and adored. During high school, the topic of us changing our last name and taking our new dad's last name (Perez) was raised for the first time. We gave it a lot of thought and initially, I loved the idea. I couldn't wait to get rid of my last name. However, the reality was that if dad (Tony) were to adopt me and Jay, our father Brad would be released of any parental responsibility. This would include the child support he was paying. It wasn't a ton of money: $385 per month for both me and Jay. It was more the principle that he was made to do the right thing — especially after he was so adamant that he wasn't going to be involved. Every time that $385-per-month came out of his paycheck he'd be reminded that he had children. We hadn't had any contact with our brother Luke, and our resentment for our father grew. So, having dad adopt was out of the question. We were going to make Brad pay, one way or another.

★   ★   ★

High school was a bit of a blur, but I do remember it being a time when I was the most embarrassed.

I was over 300 pounds when I started high school, and kids certainly didn't get sweeter. Their comments and antics just became crueler. They tried to trip me in the hallway, and they would laugh when my desk became so tight it was unbearable. They would stand in groups in the hall just waiting for me to walk by so they could get loud and obnoxious and laugh. My early childhood was still with me, and I hadn't dealt with any of it. I bottled it up and tried to lock it away, but it surfaced through my eating.

My parents tried to help. They didn't disallow me from eating anything, but they did try to give friendly nudges. My mother was introducing me to every diet plan known to man. I truly believe she did it with the best of intentions, but it never went over well with me. The more my parents tried to help, the more defiant I would become.

"They never went through what I went through, I don't need their damn help," I thought.

I never went to any high school dances or functions. I would always watch Jay making plans with friends for prom or whatever event it might be, but I just watched. I desperately wanted to go and be involved in all of those things, too, but who wants to ask the biggest girl in school to a dance? Nobody I knew. I never went to a football game because it would require getting up on the bleachers and hoping I could make my way down the aisle. I never wanted to try because I knew it wouldn't go well. A few times, I remember I would just sit outside next to the fence so I could still hear the "Thunderbird" chants for our team: "Go, team, go." I never actually saw a football game — only listened to a few of them.

Sports were something I never did either. There were two reasons. One was the fact I was so big. Even if I had been interested in a sport, the teasing was bad enough that all I could think about was what kind of backlash I would get. The second reason was that my right leg was still a source of pain even many years later. By this time, it was bowing pretty bad. My mom did take me to the doctor, and I was diagnosed with "water on the knee." The doctor said I would grow out of it. I remember thinking, "How the hell long is this going to take?" I never took any P.E. classes and ended up taking bowling just so I could have P.E. credits to graduate.

I picked up smoking when I turned 16. My parents didn't like it, but I was working and making my own money. Plus, both of my parents smoked, so it was more difficult for them to tell me to stop. The only thing they said when they found out was, "We aren't going to buy your cigarettes!" I remember chuckling a bit because I never expected them to. I had older friends for that.

Smoking seemed nice at first because I wasn't eating nearly as often. It seemed like a great solution to my "growing" problem. Every time I would get hungry, I would just grab a diet Pepsi and smoke. It worked for a while. Smoking did have a way of curbing my appetite because I had something else to do with my hands. But it wasn't a long-term solution.

The job I got when I turned 16 was fantastic because it kept me productive and busy. But, it was at a Jack in the Box fast-food restaurant. It had some of the best sourdough burgers, curly fries and milkshakes that I now had access to whenever I worked. I don't remember a single working day where I didn't eat fries and drink milkshakes. Easy access meant I was going to eat it. If something happened at school that day, I would bathe my problems in curly fries, teriyaki bowls and chocolate cake. The more weight I gained, the more comments I would receive and the more I ate.

It was during this time — my sophomore year — that we got a call out of the blue. Jay answered the phone. It was Luke. He wanted to see us. I couldn't believe it. We hadn't heard a word for over three years and then one day he said, "Hey, it's your brother."

We drove down to pick him up, and we spent the day catching up. We never resumed a normal twice-a-month visitation. I don't think Brad or Shelly was very fond of the idea of us spending time with our brother. Anytime we'd see him, we were only allowed on the front lawn. I did see Brad a few times during those times, but there was never anything more than simple formalities: "Hello" and "Goodbye." Luke was almost 15 and getting to the point where he could make his own decisions. But it was clear a lot had happened during those three years. Luke had experienced trauma. With the bitterness of his own personal experiences, the custody and things said on both sides, it wasn't quite the same. Understandably so.

For me, there was a bit of a grieving process because of this.

Luke wasn't the cute, giggly brother I had remembered. He was hard, bitter, empty.

During high school, I only saw Brad a few times. Most times it was in passing when we were dropping off Luke. He never inquired as to how we were, never asked about our lives. Luke had told me that my name wasn't allowed to be said in their home. When people asked Brad and Shelly about their kids, they only talked about the five boys. It felt as if I had been erased. That feeling was confirmed when I accidentally ran into my grandparents (Brad's parents) one time during a trip to pick Luke up at a local store. They had a light conversation with Jay, but it was clear that neither of them wanted anything to do with me. Although I was standing right next to Jay, they never said a word to me.

What in the hell had I done that was so damn terrible that even my grandparents wouldn't talk to me anymore? I tried desperately to understand it, to deal with my family erasing my existence, but I just didn't know how to cope. I didn't know how to process any of it. I didn't know what I had done. Month after month, it haunted me. And the more it haunted me, the more I ate.

If I just left Washington, my problems would go away, I thought. So, I made plans to get out.

I felt like an embarrassment. In high school, I was a good kid and never got in trouble, in fact, I did fairly well in school and had no problems getting accepted into college. However, college wasn't what I wanted to do. Jay had decided to enter the Air Force. I was devastated because I couldn't go with him. That was my first choice. I wanted nothing more than to wear a uniform, too, but there was no chance of that with my weight. I chose to go to college instead. I did it because I felt that was the only option.

I hated my life, and I hated myself. I knew I wanted out of Washington, but reluctantly chose to go to school in Texas because dad had family here.

Being in Texas — and not in Washington — did little to change my life.

I thought about Shelly regularly.

My growing hatred for this woman only seasoned with time. In high school, me and Jay used to talk about driving down to her and Brad's house to beat the crap out of her. But once I left, these plans only magnified. I kept a diary, and I had pages and pages of future plans to hurt her. By now, I didn't want to kill her, necessarily, but I wanted her to bleed. I wanted her to suffer. I literally wanted to hit her and beat her so badly that there was a good chance she might not walk again. I got satisfaction knowing that one day, justice would come. And if I had anything to do with it, it would be by my hand. Our plans were always pretty specific but not necessarily creative. We would talk about ringing the doorbell and hiding so she couldn't see us. Then, as soon as she would open the door, we would beat the living shit out of her.

Moving down to Texas didn't make those feelings go away. I knew it was only a matter of time. We were going to do it.

A year later, I was struggling in Texas. My school needed some insurance information from Brad, so I had to make the phone call to Shelly so I could get it. When I called their home, Shelly's oldest son answered the phone.

"Hey, can I talk to Shelly? I need to get some information from her."

"Athena, who did you need to talk to?"

"Shelly."

"Um, did you not know?"

"Not know what?"

"Athena, mom passed away about nine months ago."

"What?"

I quickly hung up the phone. I was in utter shock. Nobody called to let us know Shelly had passed away? Not any member of my family, not my father, not anyone?

I went into a screaming fit. I was so angry at the world for so many reasons. I wasn't upset that Shelly died. I don't mean to sound cruel, but at the time I felt no sadness for her death. I was never going to get that chance to put that woman in jail. I had been determined to lock that woman away for the rest of her life, and God took that opportunity away from me. It felt so unfair. How do you get closure with someone who's dead?

# LESSON 7

*We have to accept that some chapters in our lives have to close without closure. It's normal to have an innate desire to tell someone how they've hurt you. The anger you feel is natural.*

*A lack of closure can feel like a setback in the healing process, but getting closure requires the cooperation of all parties. We must ask ourselves if closure will resolve a traumatic experience even if we have the opportunity to get it.*

*In theory, closure will allow us to move on, but that's an illusion. We assume some final conversation is going to tie up every loose end and presto! We're healed. I don't think it's that simple. If we've been hurt, that hurt never goes away, even if things are ultimately rectified. The pain can remain.*

*The reality is that we are the only ones who can decide to be hopeful. To move forward with resolve. To feel the feelings, embrace the hurt and regret and decide to move on.*

*Closure comes from within us. It's our own self-empowered decision to move on.*

# CHAPTER 8:
## *INVITING GOD*

Shortly after explaining why I felt like I was this huge walking embarrassment to myself and my family, Jamie asked, "Are you still angry?"

They say time heals all wounds. That's a lie because if you don't deal with problems directly, they will just resurface later. Time doesn't heal wounds. Scars don't just magically disappear. Sometimes we just forget we have them. They become more like surface scabs. They're covered and temporarily forgotten, but all it would take is the slightest scratch to reopen that wound. Therapy was the scratch that opened the wounds, but I had plenty of time by this point to get out my anger.

"Not really. I can talk about it and not get mad anymore."

Shelly had been gone for years. I wasn't sure if I could cry about it anymore or not. I had gotten to the point where discussing my early childhood was getting more comfortable. The initial pain I felt during early discussions had softened a bit. My father was still alive, but I hadn't seen him in years.

"Do you still feel anger?"

"Maybe. Yes and no."

"How do you feel, Athena, about discussing this concept of forgiveness and what this might look like?"

"Absolutely not," I yelled. "It's not going to happen. I do not forgive either one of them for anything. No!"

The mere thought of forgiveness made my heart sink. You mean to tell me after all the years in this House of Horrors, I was going to have to forgive them?!

Jamie explained that forgiving them was going to be an essential part of my growth, and I needed to be open to the idea. I absolutely was not. Then again, that heaviness I felt in my heart didn't feel right either. I reluctantly told her I would at least try.

One of my first assignments was to write Brad a letter. I ended up writing a four-page note, letting him know what I thought of him, and then I promptly mailed it to him. However, this is not precisely what Jamie had in mind. The point was to get it out, but not necessarily send it. I was determined that the letter was going to have an audience. I felt terrible after I sent the letter to Brad because it didn't make me feel any better. The only thing that did make me feel better and bring some sense of peace was the fact I thought I had a voice. I felt some relief by getting it out. It was like a pot of hot water that had been boiling over for years. I was fragile. But not like a flower, more like a bomb.

A short time later, Jamie gave me an article written by the great Wayne Dyer that explained the steps in forgiveness:

1.  Turn your hurts over to God.
2.  Don't go to sleep angry.
3.  Switch the focus of blame of others to an understanding of self.
4.  Learn how to let go and be like water.
5.  Take responsibility for my part.
6.  Let go of resentments.
7.  Be kind instead of right.
8.  Don't live in the past; be present.
9.  Embrace dark times.
10. Refrain from judgment.
11. Send love.

It was a difficult list. Some of the items seemed utterly impossible. But I promised Jamie I would try, so I took the list home. I am the kind of girl that starts at the top and works her way down, so I had to attack the first one: "Turn your hurts over to God." How was I supposed to do that?

I hadn't talked to God in years. What did I need to do, pray? I had spoken to God many times in my life up to that point and don't ever recall anything good happening. Why was he going to listen to me now? I was a little irritated at the assignment because none of it made any sense.

Fine. Fine! I would pray about it.

I was a blubbering mess that night. I couldn't tell you everything I talked to God about, but I do remember a few things. I spoke about Brad a lot. Shelly was gone, but I still had this man I needed to make peace with. I didn't understand why he had erased me. How can any man just pretend one day that he doesn't have a daughter? How can any man watch a child be abused and turn a blind eye? I yelled at God and told him that when I had prayed as a young girl for my father to love me, he never answered. I just wanted Brad to be a father, and it never happened.

I must have fallen asleep because that's typically what happens. I cry myself sleepy. It was common for me to have very vivid dreams. I had dreams my whole life of various things. They were so clear and colorful, and I could remember every single detail upon waking.

But this night was different. I honestly don't know if I was awake or dreaming but there was someone at the foot of my bed. I couldn't see his face, but there was a figure. I knew it was a man only by voice.

"Athena, don't be afraid. Can you hear me?" the voice said.

"I am not afraid. Yes, I can hear you, you are sitting on my bed. What are you doing on my bed?"

"Were you not provided everything you asked for?"

"I don't know what you mean."

"I answered you. Did I not provide everything you asked for"?

I was about to ask what he meant a second time, but then, all of a sudden, I was seeing a movie in my head about my dad, Tony. I saw the first time I met him, the day he walked down the aisle with my mom. I saw him driving the family boat while we were out throwing crab pots into the water. I saw him sitting on the floor opening Christmas presents, and the day he was trying to teach me how to drive a stick and how I laughed till my sides hurt. I saw the day he was with me when I bought my first car. It went on for several minutes, and then it just stopped.

Either I woke up or the figure disappeared. I sat there in shock for several minutes because I could swear it was real. Was it a dream or did it really happen? Whether it was real or not, the message was crystal clear.

I did ask God when I was young for my dad to love me. My dad had loved me unconditionally since the day he met me. God had answered my prayers for a dad. He had been with me the whole time. I asked in that same prayer as a child for the beatings to stop. My dad never laid a finger on me. His fingers never touched me out of anger or hate. Only hugs to comfort me when I was upset or to hug me when he was proud.

I lay in bed teary-eyed. The wonderful relationship I had with my dad wasn't Brad. It was even better than what I could have imagined. It felt almost as if it were God's way of saying, "Hey, I couldn't help with this, but I could help here." I had a dad who loved me unconditionally.

I hadn't realized it until that very moment, but yes, God had answered my prayer as a little girl. I did have a dad who loved me, and he was everything I had asked for.

Every part of me wanted to believe it was just a dream, but it felt so real. I wasn't sure I would even be able to tell people. They might think I had lost my mind. But even today, I can still describe the voice, the love and warmth I felt as this man spoke.

The following day I was out running errands and stopped at my favorite little coffee shop. I had been talking with this girl who worked there for at least a year or better, making small talk and getting to know her.

I drove up to the window to get my coffee, and out of nowhere I said, "Hey, I know this is an odd question to ask through a coffee shop drive-through window, but do you know a good church around here?" Looking back, I am not sure why I wanted to go to church. I thought that maybe going to church could give me direction. Maybe going to church could confirm a miracle?

She smiled.

"Yeah! I go to a great church! I will email you the name and address."

I couldn't stop thinking about "the dream." I wasn't sure what to call it. I didn't even care, but I knew it was something I needed to hear at that moment. I knew if God could help with the first item on the list, he might be willing to help me with the rest of it. At the time, I thought the best place to find God was at church, so that's where I went. It was worth a try.

I never thought I would have an interest in attending church again. When I left the Mormon Church when I was 12, I didn't ever want to go back. But now as an adult with adult eyes, I was willing to give everything a second chance.

I tried several churches: a Baptist church, a Buddhist church, I even went back to several Mormon services. Nothing felt right. I figured I would give my coffee-shop-drive-through friend's church a try. It was a nondenominational Christian church, and Easter Sunday happened to be my first visit.

It was a beautiful service, and I even liked the songs. It wasn't much like the very conservative Mormon Church services I remember; instead, it had handclapping, upbeat music with a band! It went against everything I grew up with, but I found myself going back for more.

On my second or third visit, I heard something I will never forget. It was a talk on forgiveness. The church put a scripture up on a screen from Matthew 6:15: "But if you do not forgive men their trespasses, neither will your Father forgive your trespasses."

Forgiveness wasn't going to be dependent on whether Brad and Shelly were sorry. This was going to be a mission all my own.

"How much good can you really do with your life if every thought you have is resentful? God will not be able to use you, he will not be able to bless you. Resentment will sour your thoughts and your spirit. Forgiving someone who wronged you is completely your responsibility and not the responsibility of the person who wronged you," the pastor said.

It felt like a big job — an unfair one at that. I would have to be the forgiver. That part never sat right with me. But the part I took away most was the scripture quote from Matthew 6:15. It made me remember how imperfect I was. Yes, I would need to figure out a way to forgive them because I knew I had hurt other people along the way. Are you perfect Athena? No. Have you done no one any harm? That was a big fat "no."

It resonated. I can't say I left the services that day knowing how I was going to do it, but I knew I would need God's help.

Shortly after these first couple of services, I asked Jamie how I would know when Brad and Shelly were forgiven.

"When you are able to put yourself in their shoes," she replied.

Her response just made it 10 times harder.

"Put myself in their shoes!" I blurted out. "Are you shitting me? Impossible!"

I couldn't believe it. I walked out of her office feeling so confused and anxious that day. I flung open my car door, threw myself into my seat, slumped down and started crying. How was this going to happen? My head just sank down into my hands.

After that, I slowly started immersing myself in scripture. A part of me knew if God was going to help me master Dyer's list, I was going to need to strengthen my relationship with him. I was a scared mouse in the beginning. If a friend proves over and over she can't be trusted, or she disappears when you need her most, chances are you might not stay friends. Or, at a minimum, you might be apprehensive about asking for help if you knew she was going to let you down.

I recognized God showed me something incredibly special with my Dad Tony, and I was extremely grateful. But I wasn't exactly trusting of him yet.

★   ★   ★

"Athena, you don't speak about Texas very fondly. Didn't you like living there?" Jamie once asked.

"No, I hated it"

"You didn't like it even when you first got there?

"No."

"So, you are off to college and away from your parents, independent, you had a new life and you hated it even from Day 1? What happened Athena?"

I sat there in my comfy chair like I always did, wrapped up in that red velvet blanket with my coffee in hand. I could already feel my eyes welling up. I had been in therapy for quite a long time already, so I knew at that point she hit a nerve and it was something that we needed to talk about. I started understanding that if something brought quick tears, then it was still unresolved for me.

# LESSON 8

*Turn it over to God.*

*I know this might sound crazy to some of you, and initially, it sounded crazy to me as well. "Let Go and Let God." What if it's not just a big cliché? What if?*

*The more you lean on God during trials, the more you are welcoming Him into your life. If you're plagued by fear or worry, prayer is the best antidote (Philippians 4:6-7). It's also a surprising gift and it's difficult for me to reconcile any other truth. It has some shockingly gratifying consequences.*

*Don't ever think your difficulties are too insignificant for God to handle — He wants us to pray about everything. And then let go of your troubles and place them in God's hands. It's a big step and it's scary. I get it. But what do you have to lose?*

# CHAPTER 9:
## *SHAME*

Texas was — a shock.

I disliked it, to say the least.

I hated the weather. All the vegetation looked dead, and there were no big evergreen trees. Instead, there were cockroaches and fire ants. Aside from the fact there were some palm trees, this wasn't the escape to paradise I had in mind. I had no friends and even the family I was around I didn't know very well. The only thing that made the transition tolerable was Jay.

Jay was at basic training at Lackland Air Force Base. We essentially arrived in Texas at the same time. When I left Washington, he was on a flight headed for basic training, which just so happened to be in the same town. Typically, it's not like you can walk over to the base and say hello while they're in basic training. You don't get to see them until the day they graduate. But, me and Jay were schemers. We figured out a creative way to see each other. There was a church on base that anyone could go to on Sundays. He and a few friends would sit in the back of the church, and I would meet up with him. We had to keep it quiet, and I was never able to make a big deal when I saw him, but oh, was I excited to see him! Occasionally, I would bring McDonald's, and Jay, a few of his friends and I would all sit in the back of the church eating quarter pounders with cheese.

I started losing weight shortly after I arrived, but it was purely accidental. I arrived in July, so the weather was at its hottest. I didn't want to eat. All I wanted to do was lay around and drink water. I was miserable, and all I could think about was going back home.

★   ★   ★

I started hanging out with my cousins and their group of friends. It was fun initially, but I didn't feel part of the group. It wasn't because they weren't trying to include me. I was a bit younger  and not old enough to drink. Nearly everyone in their group was almost four years older than me, so when we went out, I was usually the designated driver. We went to clubs, but as usual, I was normally the quiet one sitting at the bar watching everyone get stupid. I didn't really know how to act or be. I felt odd and out of place. Displaced was how I always felt. No fault of theirs.

Within about four months, I had lost almost 80 lbs. I was around 295 pounds or so. I was feeling better and was definitely moving around better. I made two friends. We didn't exactly hang out after class or anything, but I had people to hang out with while I was there. My friends were Venus and

Zeus. What are the odds, seriously? In fact, I thought both of them were pulling my leg until I made them show me their driver's licenses.

One night, the cousins were having a big get together, and I was invited. This was the night I met Mark. He had too much to drink that night, and I offered to give him a ride home since he only lived a few blocks from me. I thought he was harmless, just drunk, so I didn't have a problem dropping him off on my way home.

It's amazing how quickly he sobered up because halfway home he seemed fine. He was talking up a storm, asking about me, my life. He said he wanted to show me this really cool rock formation, and I was game. We drove down this long dark road for what seemed forever before we got there.

There was no rock formation. There was nothing at the end of the road. It was a dead end. There were no houses I could see, and it seemed to be just a dense wooded area with oak and pecan trees. We stood outside the car looking at the dark scenery, then I opened the passenger side door, got in, and sat quietly waiting till he had seen enough so I could take him home.

Initially, it was fine. Mark wasn't exactly sober and was trying to make conversation, but he was a bit out of it. He started moving closer and closer to where I was sitting. I didn't know him that well, so I wasn't sure if his behavior was normal. In the middle of one of his sentences, he just stopped talking and leaned over to me like he was trying to kiss me.

Shocked, I looked at him and asked, "What are you doing?" He must have thought I was kidding because he started laughing and grabbed the back of my head and smooshed my face up to his. I was getting uncomfortable by this point because it wasn't invited. When I tried to push him away, he batted at my hands. In a playful way at first, but then he suddenly became extremely aggressive. I couldn't tell if he was playing rough or getting serious, but I didn't like it. I slapped at him to get him out of the doorway, and then he started yelling gibberish. He grabbed my hair and started yelling at me in incomplete sentences. I was big, but he was definitely stronger because I wasn't able to pull my arm back away from him. He started climbing on top of me and now I was really not having fun. I wasn't crying but I was alarmed. I wanted out of there that minute.

When I said I was going to hit him if he didn't get off of me, I felt his cold right hand grab my neck.

"Shut the fuck up," he told me.

He said he carried a pocket knife and would slit my throat if I hit him or started screaming. I had seen a man beat the crap out of my mom; I didn't want that to be me — bloody and a face so puffy her eyes were swollen shut. I didn't feel like I was going to win, so I just laid there while he did his thing. Five or six minutes later it was over. I was stunned. He told me to get out of the car, which I did, and get back into the driver's seat so I could take him home because he was tired.

During that drive he told me that if I ever told my family or cousins what happened, he would tell everyone, "You asked for it." The mere thought of my cousins finding out was the last thing I wanted. I had just moved to Texas, I didn't know anyone other than them, and he had known them his whole life. Who would they believe? I certainly didn't think it was going to be me, so I kept quiet. I would rather keep quiet than have my family believe I was some kind of whore.

"How did you feel after that happened?" Jamie asked.

"I was angry. I wasn't doing very well at all. I had only been in Texas a few short months; this was not exactly how I thought my first time would all go down."

"Did you ever see Mark again?"

"Yeah, I saw him all the time."

"All the time? What do you mean?"

I was friends with Ron, Mark's brother. So, naturally, I still saw Mark. Mark never said anything, never talked about that night. In fact, he acted like nothing ever happened. I was young at the time and very naive. I thought that's what I was supposed to do. I suppose I could have just said goodbye to that whole circle of people. It's what I should have done, but I didn't. I craved acceptance and didn't want to feel like I was alone. If I stopped hanging out with my cousins and their friends, I would have no one. It wasn't something I could deal with at the time.

I moved on and tried to forget it ever happened. But it didn't work. That desire to keep it under wraps surfaced as pure rage — lashing out at anyone and everyone. I did many things during this time I am not proud of. But I was wounded several times over.

Ron, his girlfriend, and their little circle of friends weren't exactly what I would call the best influences. Initially, they introduced me to weed. I liked it, it made me laugh. I was getting invited to every function, and they were all excited to see me. I liked this life. For once, it finally felt good. I was reluctant when they poured a line of white powder on the table, but I tried that too. I wasn't strong enough to say "no" back then. For a few weeks, I thought I had found a magic weight-loss powder. It made me stay up for 36 hours, I got tons of stuff done and I didn't want to eat. This was perfect.

I got so involved in this new circle, I forgot about my cousins, my life, school and my job. My cousin had worked hard to get me a job where he was working. But I was so messed up, I kept coming in late. I eventually left, but I think I was close to getting fired. I was flunking school, and I didn't care. I was coming home at 3 a.m. and pissing off my aunt, and I didn't care. I knew why she cared, though. She knew that circle well. I should have listened to her, but I didn't. She didn't want me part of what she saw coming, but I was defiant. I wasn't going to have anyone telling me what to do. I was paying rent, I was an adult, and I could do whatever the hell I wanted. And I did. I would eventually move out of my aunt's house due to constant bickering and tension. I ended up getting an apartment with Ron and his girlfriend, and I finally felt free. Everything was glorious for a while. I must admit things were fun. That's what I wanted: lots and lots of fun.

I came home early from work one day. I wasn't feeling too hot. I sluggishly carried myself up the stairwell to our apartment, ready to call it an early day. I opened the door, and I was horrified. Ron and one of his other brothers were counting money — more money than I had ever seen in my life. Next to the money were several bags of white powder. I knew what it was. This is exactly what my aunt was warning me about. This wasn't fun anymore. I called my parents and told them to bring the truck and come get me. That was the last day I saw Ron or any of that circle. I got an apartment of my own in a different part of town. It wasn't any bigger than my current living room, but I was happy and on my own, and trying diligently to live peacefully and put my life back together from the seeming chaos I had gotten myself into.

"Did you ever seek therapy or deal with your rape or talk to anyone about it?" Jamie asked.

"No, I never talked to anyone. Just pushed it somewhere in the back of my mind so that I didn't have to think about it."

"Did you ever think about it?"

"Sometimes. Mostly I just tried to keep myself busy so that I wouldn't have to."

"Athena, you mentioned that you were angry at your mom for staying with John for a while, even after he beat her."

"Yes, I was terribly angry. Who the HELL does that?"

"Well, you did."

"What do you mean!?"

"A man rapes you, and you were too afraid to leave that circle of people, so you stayed. Staying meant you still had to see him, you were still around him."

I stared at Jamie.

I suppose she was right. I never understood how my mom could possibly go back to someone who hurt her. But that's exactly what I did. For the first time, sitting there in Jamie's office that day, I understood how fear can make you do things you don't want to do. It can keep you someplace you don't want to be. It was eye-opening. It was a level of understanding that someone could only be empathetic about if they'd been there. Some of those childhood resentments I had about John and my mom seemed to disappear that very day. Like a light bulb had gone off in my brain somewhere.

"So, you didn't talk about it with anyone. Were there positive things to keep you busy at that time?"

"I am not sure how positive they were, but it kept my mind off it."

"Like what?"

For a while, I got on the weight loss train. It was just work and school, so I had lots of downtime to work on the weight. I was 19 by this time, and I didn't care how I had to do it. If I could have cut it off, I would have — regardless of any pain involved. I was an all-or-nothing kind of person, so I plunged in headfirst. My daily diet consisted of water, a can of tuna and a can of green beans. I was working out like a madwoman, going to the gym sometimes several times a day. Within eight weeks, I had dropped nearly 60 lbs. Some might say that was drastic. It was, but, damn, I felt great. I could fit into a pair of 18 jeans, and it was the lowest I had ever been in my life.

Suddenly guys were everywhere. Initially, it was marvelous. I was going on dates and having all kinds of experiences that previously were a locked door for me. Men that had known me months earlier were now asking me out on dates.

But I didn't react to it all in a positive way. I wasn't happy anymore. I was angry and resentful.

Wasn't I the same person months earlier? I didn't like the feeling of being smaller. I felt like I was losing my security blanket. As odd as that sounds, it was a very real sensation for me. If the weight were gone, what could I possibly hide behind? It wasn't something conscious — only feelings. I didn't want to lose any more weight. It was making me feel uncomfortable. Initially, I thought losing weight would bring happiness and my life would be perfect, but that's not what it brought. I lost interest in losing weight, and most of my free time was spent dating. Over the next year-and-a-half I had several boyfriends, Fiancé No. 1, breakups, a pregnancy and a miscarriage when I was five weeks along. I was only 20 when it happened. I was dating a guy in the Air Force and had driven up to Ellsworth Air Force Base to surprise him one weekend and found him with another woman. I was devastated, as you can imagine, and even more panicked when I found out I was pregnant. I felt bad that I was happy when I miscarried. I wouldn't say elated, but it brought a sense of relief. I wasn't ready to have children. Part of my relief was the lifestyle. I was having far too much fun being single, dating and going to school. I didn't have time for children.

"So, you were never upset about losing someone that cheated, and you lost a baby?" Jamie asked. "You weren't upset about losing that baby?"

"I thought about it. But no, I wasn't ready."

"Athena, did you ever consider that possibly Brad and Shelly weren't ready for you?"

This was something I had never considered. But there was validity in the question. It left me something to ponder that day. When Brad and Shelly married, they were both young: 27-years- old. They were both single parents with three small children. In the Mormon religion, you get married, you don't stay single — at least, that was my perception. I am sure they were both getting a lot of pressure from both of their families to find someone and settle down. I am sure they both heard it: "Shelly, you need a father for those boys." And, "Brad, you need a mother for those kids." No doubt, they heard something similar to that. Did I believe Brad and Shelly had been ready to come together with six children? No, not at all. I think it definitely could've been the catalyst that popped something loose in both their heads. All I know is that neither one of them was the same once they got married. People called us the "Bradley bunch." Perhaps it's really that simple: They weren't ready. That could have all kinds of ramifications in terms of stress, decisions and sanity.

I remember thinking about this question many times. Perhaps it was just that simple. Maybe they just snapped.

# LESSON 9

*By Athena Perez with Chase Knight*

George Bernard Shaw, in 1925 said, "Those who cannot change their minds cannot change anything."

*Our perspectives and narratives come in many forms. Maybe it's the tiny voice in our head. What about society's influence on how we think? Perhaps it's our assumptions because we lack information. But what we fail to realize is that the repetitive nature of whatever dialogue we hear or choose to hear will influence our perceptions. Being objective when we are emotionally connected is difficult but possible.*

*We can be the reason for our own misery. When we continuously tell ourselves something over and over, it's inevitable that we will believe whatever it is that's being said. It's not a simple undertaking, but the ability to change our mind requires fluidity, willingness to understand and extreme self-awareness.*

# CHAPTER 10:

## *RESENTMENT*

Shortly before my 21st birthday, I met a guy named Nick. He was an officer in the U.S. Armed Forces. I couldn't figure out what he saw in me. I was very much plus-sized, still hovering around the 240s. He was slim, fit, very athletic — my complete opposite in every sense of the word. He was a first-generation American so we had cultural differences, and our upbringings couldn't have been more different. He already had several degrees by this time and was making plans for law school. I thought he'd be the stability I was looking for.

The first two years of our relationship were peaceful, active and quite fun-filled. Peace has a funny way of bringing silence to trauma. When things are good, you can forget about almost anything.

We traveled extensively, from Texas to the East Coast and the Bahamas.

After we had been dating for over two years, I wanted to know where the relationship was going. So, one day, I asked him how he felt.

"Athena, I can't marry you until you get your weight off."

It was a devastating blow. He met me at the same weight; nothing had changed. It wasn't like he met me at a size two, and suddenly, I had put on a bunch of weight. I hadn't realized it bothered him so much. But if this was the case, why was he with me? He had a lot of reasons, but ultimately he told me he was not going to put a ring on my finger until I reached a size 12. I am not sure where that magic size came from other than I do believe his mother was a size 12.

I tried hard to make that happen. I really did. The pressure was intense, and subconsciously I am sure I fought it every step of the way. If I put something in my mouth he didn't approve of, he'd make sure I got a dirty look. I remember glaring back at him, thinking, "Watch this, you jerk." I would put whatever he didn't want me eating in my mouth. I hated that he was controlling my food. Hated it. My solution was to hide it from him. I ate whatever I wanted whenever he wasn't around. Nick was kicking up quite a bit of old memories with food control. His good intentions — if you could call them that — were a very bitter reminder of my past. Something I had fought to forget. I didn't like being told what I could eat.

If the pressure to lose weight wasn't enough, he kept trying to pressure me into going to the gym. Physical activity wasn't something I ever did because every time I would try to run or do fair amounts of even walking, my right leg still hurt. One day, he took me to the gym and told me to get on the treadmill because he was going to teach me how to run. I made it about three-quarters of a mile and told him I needed to stop. He got a bit irritated with me.

"Athena, you need to push through the pain. Stop being weak. You are weak!"

I couldn't understand why everyone ran if it hurt so badly. Push through the pain? How? I got back on the treadmill and tried to keep going but I could feel tears running down my face.

"You are weak!"

I couldn't do it. I guess I was weak and maybe I had a low tolerance for pain.

Nick made me feel so bad all the time. But I tried so hard to please him. Many times, I would just get on the treadmill and cry through it. It was utter misery.

Our culture clashes also became a problem. Two years after we met, I was finally allowed to go with him to meet his family. I was excited. I was excited until I was actually standing on his father's front porch. His father met us at the door, walked outside and spit on me. In his culture, spitting on someone meant the worst of the worst. It was like saying "you are no better than the spit on the bottom of my shoe." It was the worst insult you could give someone. I wasn't from his culture and his family didn't approve. They were speaking in their native tongue so I wouldn't understand what they were saying. They were abrasive and they kept pointing at me. We stayed at a hotel that weekend instead of his family's home.

I couldn't change the color of my skin or alter the fact I was born in America. I didn't want to throw away two years, so I kept saying to myself, "Things will get better. They will come around eventually."

The fact I did not feel welcomed by this family made me feel terrible. I had struggled with acceptance most of my life. What had I done? Nothing. I was American, and, at that time, I had no degree. They believed he deserved better and wanted him to marry into his own culture. I struggled with the brashness but believed in my heart that if they got to know me, they would like me. If they saw I loved Nick and wanted nothing more than to be good for him, they would see that.

Credit wise, I was a sophomore in college. I was still going to school, but it was a struggle because I was also working full-time. School was part-time, at best. Coming up with tuition and book money was always difficult.

"I am not helping you with any of your schooling," Nick told me.

When I asked him why, he said, "You could've gone to a military academy as well and had all of your tuition covered. But you couldn't get in because you are heavy. That's your fault and your responsibility, so I am not helping you."

I was heartbroken but tried to rationalize his statement. Yes, it was true: I couldn't go into the military or the academies because I wouldn't have passed the physical requirements. He wasn't wrong here, but it didn't mean I wasn't in tears. He also made comments about me being behind in my education.

"Athena, you graduated high school seven years ago. You should have your masters by now."

He was right. But it hurt when he said it. If anything in the relationship wasn't going perfectly, he took shots at me. I don't know whether it was supposed to make me feel bad or whether it was a twisted way of trying to motivate me. It always made me feel awful. There were many times when I was glad it was Sunday evening because he would be leaving, or I would be going home. I will admit there were times I was glad to be rid of him for a few days. Nick still wasn't budging on his promise not to marry me until the weight was off. I felt like my life was on hold until I could lose the weight. I couldn't make any plans to be his wife, I couldn't talk about our future, I couldn't do anything until that magic size 12 appeared.

I was only 24 years old but felt like I had already lived a lifetime. I felt old, haggard and dragged out. I decided to leave Texas for a while so I could spend some time back home in Washington. I wanted some time to clear my head. I was stressed, I wasn't sleeping and I was depressed. It was time for a break. I was tired of Nick's size-12 conditions. Once again, he reminded me there would be no marriage until I lost the weight. This time, I had enough. I told him we were breaking up, and I made the move back to Washington for a while. I knew Shelly was gone but there was a slight hope I could mend things with my family, and perhaps, just maybe, I could have a relationship with Brad.

Two months later, I found out I was pregnant. I called Nick to tell him. He didn't react in the way I had hoped. He was yelling at me over the phone.

"Athena, you are trying to ruin my career! I don't even think it's mine! I am not helping you. You left me. You left me!"

I was mortified. I knew after this phone call that I was going to be on my own. I wasn't sure how telling him he was going to be a father would ruin his military career, but he was convinced.

It took several weeks, but I was getting more used to the idea that I was going to be a mother. I spent most of my evening hours making baby clothes on my sewing machine. My mom had taught me to sew when I was in high school, so making baby clothes became a hobby of mine. I didn't know whether I was going to have a boy or a girl, so I kept the clothing to bright yellows and greens and the patterns neutral.

I was almost 20 weeks when I woke up to severe cramping. It felt like I was being ripped apart. I called 911 and an ambulance took me to the hospital. Within an hour of arriving, doctors diagnosed me with placenta previa, which caused a premature rupture of membranes.

My son, Aidan, lived for 17 minutes and died shortly after we met due to respiratory distress syndrome. He had all of his parts and was clearly a tiny boy. Tiny hands, tiny feet, a nose no bigger than a freckle. His skin didn't look like flesh, it was almost a see-through reddish-blue, and I could see all his little veins.

I was asked if I was going to have a funeral. It seemed like it was all too much. I couldn't afford to bury him at the time and in no way was I in an emotional state to handle the arrangements on my own. I could have called one of my brothers or my parents, but I opted not to. I felt at the time it was just something I needed to handle on my own — not a wise decision.

I felt that maybe God knew I would be an abuser. They say many abused become abusers. Maybe God knew something I didn't know?

I felt like maybe there was something broken in my body. Could all those beatings and pouring rubbing alcohol where rubbing alcohol is not supposed to be poured do something to my body? Did it hurt me in ways that I wasn't aware of?

I opted not to receive his ashes. It's something I have felt terrible guilt and regret over since it happened. I essentially just walked away from it. Emotionally, it was all I could do. I only knew one thing: God wasn't real.

He couldn't possibly be. How much punishment is one girl supposed to go through? How much pain does one person deserve? I vowed I would never speak to God again, but I did remember Aidan's birthday every November 16.

After that, I threw myself into work and food and gained almost 80 pounds over the next year. I felt like a piece of my heart had died with Aidan, and it was never going to come back. I was a little less soft, a little less empathetic, a little less understanding. There was a hardness that came over me I can't describe. I was not a joyful person. I was curt, aggressive and quick-tempered. Perhaps I was giving the world way too much; it had taken far too much from me.

Two years later, I decided to go back to Texas. I missed Nick. We had gone through a lot together, and we had many years invested in our relationship. I thought I would try one more time. I decided that I would stop fighting the weight and just get it off. I wanted acceptance, I wanted him to be proud of me. I mean I didn't want to be heavy anyway. What was I fighting? I was going to have to prove I was serious about the relationship because I had gained 80 pounds while I was gone. Nick was offered a job on the East Coast and told me he would be gone for 24 months. I could wait that long. Another couple of years was no big deal. We decided to continue dating long distance. I felt like I was strong enough to make it work.

Nick had been gone on the East Coast for over two years and it didn't appear that he was coming home any time soon. We took turns flying; about every six weeks either I was flying to New York or he was flying to Texas. It made things exciting because it was fresh and new every few weeks.

That same year, I asked him how he felt about me moving to New York to be closer to him. He immediately became very defensive and told me I needed to stay in Texas to finish school and work on my weight. I could do those things anywhere. I wasn't sure why he was so against it. It was like he was punishing me for not having the weight off and for not having my degree yet.

After Nick and I had been together for nearly eight years I told him he was going to put a ring on my finger, or I was walking. He put a ring on my finger, but not how every girl dreams. It was forced. He ultimately promised he would not bother me about the weight anymore and that he would accept me as I was. As happy as I was hearing this, it never sat well because there were so many years when this was not the case. Unbeknownst to me, there were years of resentment piling up, but I continued full steam ahead with wedding plans. Our wedding date was set for early 2009.

As time passed, things became very dark. Nick came to visit for important life events, including college graduation. But, for the most part, he was absent in my day-to-day activities. I felt like I was becoming a new woman on my own. I developed interests including flying airplanes and riding motorcycles without him or anyone telling me what I should or shouldn't do, or whether they approved of my choices or diet. The more time marched on, knowing I was getting married made me feel weird. I was having a hard time mentally with the wedding because I couldn't visualize myself in my own dress.

Nick did finally come home. Six months before our wedding was scheduled. I thought initially that when he came home it would solve our problems. I believed the distance was our issue, so if he came home everything would be perfect. I was wrong.

Conversations started to feel like depositions. Nick's homecoming also came with new house rules:

1.  I was not allowed to use my mobile phone between the hours of 6 p.m. and 10 p.m.

2.  Dinner was my responsibility and it needed to be ready by 6 p.m.

3.  I needed to be up by 5 a.m. so we could go to the gym. I was required to go to the gym every day.

4.  I was not allowed to go grocery shopping alone; he wanted to be there to ensure I made the right choices.

5.  He was in charge of the finances. The last word was his because he made more money than I did.

6.  And his final new rule: This silly business I had created with Dennis needed to stop. I needed to get serious.

The above rules did not come with options. It was all or nothing.

We started going to pre-marriage counseling, but he stopped coming after the first session. I ended up doing all but one on my own. Nick got upset at the therapist who told him his new rules and attitude weren't reasonable.

During couple's therapy — or singles therapy, in my case — I thought hard about all those years alone. Everything was always what he wanted, how he wanted it, as fast as he wanted. I suddenly felt like my life was no longer my own. This didn't feel like love to me. It felt like control. Unbeknownst to me, I had become bitter and resentful.

We were four months from the wedding. Invites had already gone out and people were already booking airline tickets. I didn't know what to do. But Nick solidified my decision when he told me he wouldn't marry me unless I signed a prenuptial agreement. Our relationship crumbled, and the final straw was a houseplant.

When he asked for a prenuptial agreement, I picked up the closest thing I could find, and I threw it into the dinner he was making on the stove. Dirt went everywhere and he called the cops on me and told them I was getting violent. I regret throwing the house plant but was secretly glad his dinner was ruined. It wasn't one of my prouder moments, but mentally I had just tapped out. I just wanted him out of the house.

I felt horrible and I was embarrassed. But there was only one decision left for me: Who gets the seven houses, and who gets the furniture? We were done. I was walking away from 11 years and scared as hell, but I knew I had to.

# LESSON 10

*The damage I did by carrying around so much resentment was real. We can carry on feeling resentful. "Or we can accept our resentment, listen to the message it's trying to share with us, and adjust accordingly." -- Hannah Braime*

*Interestingly enough, resentment, fear and anger are all connected.*

*"We become trapped in a self-obsessed cycle of being afraid of the future, angry in the present, and filled with resentment over our past." -- Jessica Ruane*

*The reason resentment is so hard to deal with is because the common approaches to dealing with it are ineffective: "Just let it go" or "Just forget about it; move on." This doesn't work.*

*You need to face it, to feel it, and only then can you heal it. It's a long and painful journey, but I promise you it's worth it.*

# CHAPTER 11:
## *FEAR*

During my 11-year relationship with Nick, other things were happening in my life that I compartmentalized. I am sure this didn't help the relationship.

Fear, after all, is a terrible thing.

When I was young, I used to hear of crazy things happening to other people and think, "That only happens in the movies." Well, it doesn't.

When I was 21, I was living in a rented condo. It was nothing special, but it had cute hardwood floors and a little courtyard in the back where there was enough room for my dog.

It was an exceptionally cold winter that year in Texas, and I was having constant problems with the heat. I didn't exactly have the most responsive landlord when it came to maintenance. However, I was licensed in property management and knew a little something about his obligations to take care of problems. Three different requests to fix the heat went unanswered. I ended up going to the hospital for pneumonia.

When I turned the water on one morning to take a shower, it was yellow, and it had a mixture of sand and rock in it. I loved my place, but I couldn't live like that. I gave my notice to the landlord and moved out. Because he hadn't fixed the problems, he was supposed to refund my deposit. I knew he wasn't going to give it back, but I was so upset at this point, I would call him daily to annoy him. I figured eventually he might give up and give me my money back. The more he didn't return my letters and calls, the angrier I became.

I called the landlord on the phone one morning and told him that I was going to be out of town for a couple of weeks over Christmas visiting family. I demanded that when I returned home I had better find a check in the mail or I would sue him.

The day after I got home, I received a phone call from him.

"Athena, I have decided to give you your deposit back. Why don't you meet me over at the condo this afternoon, and I will return your money. I need you to sign a few things."

Meeting him at the condo didn't seem odd at all at the time. I had lived there for over a year. It had a beautiful countertop we could use to sign the papers. I had no concern in the world.

When I arrived, the condo was locked tight. The blinds were closed, and the door was locked. There was a light mist outside, and I didn't want to get rained on, so I walked around the fence, entered the courtyard, and sat on the back porch until the landlord arrived. I had waited over half an hour when I could hear the sounds of police radio chatter that was getting closer. I heard footsteps, so I started looking around to see what was going on. Suddenly, the back gate opened, and to my surprise, there were two deputy sheriffs.

I thought it was odd, but one of the officers looked at me and said, "Is your name Athena?"

"Yes."

With that, he lowered his hands to his belt, unclipped his handcuffs, and grabbed at my shoulder.

"Ma'am, you are under arrest."

"What?! Under arrest for what?"

"Trespassing."

I gasped in desperation and disbelief. As the officers walked me back out to the condo parking lot where the deputy sheriff police vehicle awaited me, the landlord was standing there holding paperwork. He looked at me, smiled and said, "Who outsmarted who, you little bitch?"

While I was gone, the landlord had processed an eviction on me, knowing full well that I had already vacated the unit. He had provided the courts a lease and statement that he had failed to receive rent. Because I was not in town to defend the eviction, it was granted.

In Texas, if you show up back at a place you are evicted from you can be arrested for trespassing with a nice attachment called, "habit shelter," which means you have been repeatedly asked to leave and you refuse.

It was a very well thought out plan, and he had got me. Furthermore, I could do little to defend the charge of trespassing because, in Texas, there doesn't need to be criminal intent. It was quite an elaborate setup but an easy one for the landlord to accomplish with me being out of town. All of this because he didn't want to give me my $1,000 deposit.

The police took me to jail, towed my car and treated me like a common criminal. They say you are innocent until proven guilty. This was not my experience. By the time I was released 12 hours later, I had bruises from the aggressive intake personnel. I was talked down to, insulted, and cussed at.

Because I had an eviction, I was powerless to defend the charge. I had no choice but to plead guilty. I now had a class A misdemeanor on my record. I had to do community service and check in once a week to do pee tests to make sure I wasn't on drugs.

What had I done that was so terrible? I wanted my deposit back?

Now I was pissed off. I declared war on the planet. If you crossed me, it wasn't going to end well for you. I grabbed my proverbial sword. I was ready to fight anyone.

A year later, I found myself as the plaintiff in a bitter lawsuit against the city I lived in for the actions of two police officers. Because there was a settlement agreement, I can't go into case specifics. What I can say is two police officers and two friends of theirs violated my civil rights. The police chief was included in the lawsuit because he was responsible for the actions of the officers; the department and city itself were also included because they were responsible for the department.

It didn't take long for me to feel fear. The kind of fear you only read about. To make matters worse, the police officers kept saying, "Why believe her? She has a criminal record." I felt attacked, and I was going to have to fight hard to defend my name.

I was living alone at the time of the filing, but the following day I came home to find my home had been ransacked. Every drawer in my house had been emptied, every cupboard was open and the back patio with all my furniture was turned upside down. The plants and flowers had all been uprooted. I went to the police, but what happens when you suspect the police?

I would find police department pens hanging on bushes outside my home — just silly little ballpoint pens with the police emblem on them. I would see police cars sitting on top of the hill beside my house. In five months, I had nine seat belt violations. They would sit in their police cars and wait for me to leave my driveway so they could pop me with an offense.

I came out of class one day to find all my tires had been slashed in the parking lot. This was a university parking lot with cameras. But nobody saw a thing. And footage from that hour had mysteriously disappeared.

I would break into a sweat if I saw a police car behind me as I white-knuckled the steering wheel to focus on the road. I never knew if it was a random police car just out doing his business or if this one was intended to frighten me.

My lawyers filed an anti-harassment claim against the department. It got so bad, one of my lawyers advised I skip town until the trial. This is how I ended up back in Washington for a few years.

The case was taken on by my attorney and a team of six other lawyers who viciously defended my case. Judges and cooperating lawyers called the case "Samson and Goliath." Those cases are difficult, sometimes impossible. Two other defendants were also in the lawsuit; they fled to Mexico during the depositions.

I had multiple interviews inside the offices of the U.S. Secret Service. That's right: the Secret Service. It was a living nightmare.

We were successful at taking the case all the way to the U.S. Court of Appeals for the Fifth Circuit in New Orleans, Louisiana, so there would be a fair trial away from political influence.

After six years, the city and police department said they wanted to settle. That particular year was called "the Year of Police Disgrace" by local newspapers. There was a forced resignation or "early retirement" for the police chief, both officers were fired and we got $2 million in judgments from the other two defendants. But they quickly filed bankruptcy.

The warrior had brought the city down. However, It did not give me the happy ending that I had wanted. However, it DID empower me. Not only did I have my sword, but now I had a suit of armor.

No more than two years later, I was in the middle of another lawsuit.

I was working as a project manager for a small brokerage. The broker, Steve, introduced me to a character we'll call Luigi. He always walked around in suits with white collared shirts half-buttoned down so you could see his hairy chest. He wore pointed snakeskin shoes, spoke with a heavy East Coast Italian accent and bragged about how much money he had and the big house he lived in. He rubbed me the wrong way from Day 1. He reminded me of someone you'd see in the movie, The Godfather.

Steve explained to me that he and Luigi were buying some condominiums in Georgia because they got a bargain, and they were going to rent them until they resold. He also said he was going to make almost $1 million. He always talked about making money and some big new deal he was working on, but most of the time nothing panned out. So, I never took him seriously.

A short time later, I was watching TV news reporters discussing an unstable Georgia economy.

Wait a minute. Isn't this where Steve was buying condos? Why would you want to invest in an area that was tanking? I wasn't a real estate genius, but it was starting to sound like this wasn't one of his most brilliant ideas. I even saw a few headlines in The New York Times that same day. One of them read, "As Condos Rise in South Georgia, Nervous Investors Flee."

I shrugged it off.

About a month later, I was doing some banking reconciliations and logged on to the brokerage's bank account. My eyeballs nearly popped out of my head when I saw that almost three-quarters of a million dollars had hit the bank account the night before. What in the holy hell? I called the bank immediately. They told me it was not a mistake. When I asked Steve about it, he said, "Athena, I want you to come to Georgia with me to look at these condos I just bought so you can get them rented."

Steve and Luigi started talking on the phone daily. Their deal had gone through.

We flew to Georgia and got settled into our accommodations. Steve had scheduled a meeting to talk with the appraiser. Of course, I got dragged along; I was bored out of my mind, and half annoyed because there wasn't much reason to be there. In fact, I had no interest in managing these properties, but it was part of the job description.

Shortly after we got back from meeting with the appraiser, I heard a knock on the door. I opened the door, and a man was standing there wearing a nice suit. He was clean-shaven and looked very professional. He smiled at me, introduced himself, and pulled a leather billfold from his chest. All I remember was seeing a badge and him saying, "I am with the Federal Bureau of Investigation."

I thought I was going to have a heart attack.

The agent told Steve that the condo purchase was being investigated by the FBI and that Luigi, his business partner in the deal, was being investigated for a myriad of reasons that included mortgage fraud.

The FBI asked Steve questions, and he seemed willing to talk. I had known Steve many years by this point, and I had no reason to believe he would be mixed up with shady people. He was always trying to find that pie in the sky, but never for a second did I think he would ever do anything illegal.

The agent explained he wasn't being investigated and that he was being considered a victim in the deal as long as the condo mortgage was being paid. Steve explained to the agent that his plans were to rent out the condos, and he had no intention of failing to pay the mortgages.

I was fine until we came to the part in the conversation when the agent asked Steve if he had ever spoken to the appraiser. He replied, "No."

My face went white. We had just met with the appraiser earlier that day. I didn't hear much else from the conversation because I was so alarmed. I trusted Steve. He was my friend. Why would he lie about meeting with the appraiser?

The agent got up to leave, and I showed him to the door. I knew I wanted to tell the agent what I knew, but I also knew Steve was watching me. I watched the agent walk down the hall, and I looked back at Steve who had gone to the bathroom. Now was my chance. I ran down the hallway after the agent to try and get a business card so I could call him, but he was already gone. I remember such a cloud of heaviness because I knew something wasn't right.

When we got back home after the trip, my mind was running in a million directions. I didn't have to wait long because everything started falling apart. The office phone started ringing; different law enforcement agencies were now calling the office.

I was sitting in Steve's office one day when that FBI agent called again. On this particular call, he had asked if Steve had spoken with Luigi any time recently. He replied, "No."

Once again, I knew it was a lie. Steve had spoken to Luigi several times that week alone. What in the hell was going on?

I felt like it was time to take a trip down to the FBI. Nothing smelled right.

I went and gave my statement to the FBI about things I knew and lies that had been told for what reason I hadn't a clue. The agents thanked me and told me to let them know if I came across any other information that might be helpful. I wanted out of the brokerage and wanted to quit that day, but I figured staying might be useful.

The IRS started an audit of the business a short time later. Various police officers would stop by asking for Steve, but he stopped coming to the office. For a time, I rarely saw him.

The following spring, Steve came into my office one morning and told me to stop making the mortgage payments on the Georgia condos.

"Have you lost your mind," I screamed at him. "The FBI agent told you down in Georgia that you were only going to be the victim as long as you continued to make payments. He was clear about this!"

He started yelling back at me, and a bitter argument ensued.

Once again, I went back to the FBI to give another statement. There was no way I was going to get tangled up in some scam.

The following day, I made a trip to the office to pack up my things. I was quitting, but coincidentally I got locked out of my office and was given paperwork by a new guy they had hired that stated I was being sued. Cause? Slander. They popped me with every other colorful thing they could think of as well. Preposterous.

Once again, I had to defend my name and honor. They backed up all their claims with, "Look, she has a criminal record. Who are you going to believe? Her or us?"

There were a lot of sleepless nights, lots of tears that year. I finally managed to graduate with a degree in criminal justice administration in May 2008. ironic.

This lawsuit lasted five years. It was finally dismissed before trial when the judge on the case grew increasingly impatient with Steve and his lawyer. They had made terrible claims about me but never brought any evidence to the court of wrongdoing.

The other guy, Luigi, was sentenced to 51 months in federal prison for conspiracy to commit wire fraud, followed by three years of supervised release and restitution in the amount of $1.5 million. He pled guilty. Apparently, when he learned he was being prosecuted, he fled to Europe where he had relatives. Several years later, he made the mistake of traveling to South America, where he was denied entry and forced to enter the United States. There, he was arrested by the U.S. State Department.

By the time I was 30, I had spent 14 years of my life in some form of litigation — in courts, in depositions, giving statements and wondering why this kept happening to me.

During the first case, I especially feared for my life and my safety. Where do you go for help when the people who are meant to keep you safe are the real danger? How often does this kind of thing happen? It's hard to know. But if you were to do a casual search on Google News, it would reveal a disturbing number of accounts of rogue police officers using the power of the badge to intimidate and stalk. It happens. Not just on TV.

I had experienced first-hand police indiscretion and abuse of power and dragged into one of the biggest subprime mortgage crises in history. I had hoped and believed I could have a better life. But now, the fuel had run out. I was mentally and physically exhausted. I had no fight left to give anyone. Transformation into the ice-cold warrior was complete. I had successfully warded off attack after attack. I had a sword, full armor and a lot of bitterness.

Coping mechanism: Food. It was always food.

★   ★   ★

*"The cause was within me; the effect was therefore outside of me. In order to change the effects of my life, I first needed to change their cause."* -- Greg Amundson, The Warrior and the Monk

"Athena do you believe you kept finding yourself in similar circumstances because it's what you kept putting out there? It's because it's what you keep thinking about?" Jamie asked me.

I was initially annoyed.

"You mean to tell me that somehow I was attracting these types of circumstances over and over again?"

"Well, yes, that's exactly what I am saying. You'll stop attracting certain kinds of people when you heal the part of you that once needed them. The Law of Attraction states that whatever energy you are putting out there is what will return. However, like any law, there's a positive and a negative. If you put out thoughts of abundance and gratefulness, you will attract more things to be grateful for. The same applies to the negative. If you keep experiencing bad things, then some part of you either wanted or needed these kinds of things at a very (most likely) subconscious level."

If this were true, it meant that there had been some disturbing consequences of my own thinking when it came to the experiences of my life. My weight, my circumstances, the people I attracted; everything was what I asked for whether I knew it or not.

I tried to look at some of my experiences objectively. When I had the dispute with my landlord, it made me bitter and it had me ready to fight the world. Well, guess what happened? I told the world I was ready to fight, so things I would need to fight kept showing up. Oh my gosh.

This was a huge pill to swallow. I was responsible. Saying I was overwhelmed would be an understatement. But I also felt liberated. It meant that if I could change my thoughts, I could change my life.

# LESSON 11

*By Athena Perez with Tyson Oldroyd*

*As a man thinketh in his heart, so is he (Proverbs 23:7).*

*The people or circumstances we attract into our lives have a lot to do with what we think of ourselves. If you keep asking yourself how bad circumstances are, or how unsavory people keep finding a way into your life, you're going to have to look at your own thoughts and behavior as the primary source of this complicated "attraction."*

*We have the ability to turn off the negativity, which is our greatest blessing. We can choose to approach an unfortunate situation with a positive mindset. When bad things happen, we can make the choice to look at our situations with positive expectancy and believe that whatever is happening to us is preparing us for a new life.*

*Things don't just happen. They happen for a reason, and most of that has to do with what we are putting out there. When armed with the right mindset, you can equip yourself better to handle life's curveballs, which will ultimately be the energy and circumstances that follow. If you welcome the negative, negative will appear. The same applies to the positive.*

# CHAPTER 12:
## NEW NARRATIVE

It had been almost three years since I started therapy.

Yet, when asked, I still had "I am" statements like these:

"I am stuck. I am fat. I am depressed. I am behind. I am unaccomplished."

It was clear to me that even though I was feeling better, the magic connections that happen when we're ready to start attacking big mountains weren't there yet. There was still a lot of bitterness that time itself had not healed. I didn't know what to do, but I did understand that I needed to get more proactive in my healing. I was becoming aware that the things I thought about the most were creating my reality, but I wasn't sure how to fix it.

I was being prompted to read, so I bought my first self-help book, The Four Agreements, by Don Miguel Ruiz. It was a rather revealing little book that explains the source of self-limiting beliefs that rob us of joy and create needless suffering.

The four agreements as written by Ruiz are:

1. Be impeccable with your word. This means to speak with integrity but only say what you mean. Avoid using words to speak badly about others, but avoid using any words that speak badly of yourself. Use your words for love.

2. Don't take anything personally. What other people say and do has nothing to do with you. When others speak, they are only projecting their own reality or their own wants and dreams. When you are immune to the opinions and actions of others, you won't be the victim of needless suffering.

3. Don't make assumptions. Have the courage to express how you feel and ask for what you want. Communicate with others clearly so you can avoid misunderstandings.

4. Always do your best. Your best will not be the same every day. In fact, your best can change from day to day. For instance, when you are sick, your best will not be as good as a healthy day. Under all circumstances just do your very best and avoid self-abuse, regrets, and self-judgment.

I loved the book but struggled with the practical application. I had to read the book three times before I was able to understand some of the things I had done.

Being impeccable with my word meant others wouldn't have the power to tear me down. Were the words I was using creating who I wanted to be? Absolutely not. Did the words "fat," "depressed," "isolated," "alone," and "unaccomplished" create a belief in myself? Once again, absolutely not. Unbeknownst to me, these words became my belief system, and I had made a steadfast decision about who I was based on the simple words I used to describe myself. Unfortunately, they had become words I believed, and that was the saddest part. I had done it to myself.

There was also an incredible realization about my past. The abuse I suffered and hurtful situations in my life I had to endure didn't always have anything to do with me. I had made huge assumptions. Shelly's opinion of me became my own personal view of myself. I had assumed she did all these things because she didn't like me. There could have been a thousand other reasons that had nothing to do with me. I had assumed Chris killed himself because of me. Again, there were probably a thousand other reasons. I always assumed that because I saw myself as fat; everyone else saw me that way. All of these assumptions became the way I saw myself.

I was harder on myself than anyone out there slinging dirt at me. I said more mean things about myself than any other person in the world. I had disappointed myself hundreds of times and punished myself for it. I had been punishing myself for years, far longer than any time I had spent with Shelly. Was it truly my life I needed help with, or was it really me that was the problem? I did this to myself.

"We are addicted to anger, jealousy, and self-pity," Ruiz wrote.

I was angry, I was jealous and I was definitely doing some serious self-pitying.

I recognized my mind was a big problem. I was going to have to learn how to look at myself differently. I knew that would be tough. So many years of bad self-talk. How do I just erase that? Was it possible? Mind, body, spirit. It was the first time I understood how important that trifecta is. If I truly wanted to feel better and conquer this weight problem, it was going to take a combination of all three if I were going to be successful, especially long term.

But then came the tough part. I didn't exactly know how just to magically look at myself differently. It was going to require new self-talk, new affirmations I could practice daily. This took some work at the start. I never had a routine or something I did every single day without fail. Most days

I just winged it.

In a valiant effort the following morning, I found myself staring blankly into the bathroom mirror.

"Athena, you are beautiful. No, you aren't. You are a big fat cow," I screamed as I slammed the mirror.

Now I had a crack running all the way down the center of the mirrored cabinet. I was going to have to buy a new one. I started bawling. I didn't care about the cabinet. I was frustrated. This voodoo shit I was doing was stupid. How was I ever going to get to the point where I could look in the mirror and say, "Athena, you are beautiful. Athena, you are worth it. Athena, you are special," and actually believe it? I couldn't even fathom it. It all seemed like such a big lie. I was a liar.

The affirmations weren't enough because I didn't believe a single one of them. Secondly, I disliked the practice so much that I wasn't doing them every day. I needed structure. Mostly because I had deep-seated issues with repeated behaviors. I had a weight problem because of repeated behaviors. The only way to fix this was to create new habits. How do I do that?

I found the next book I hoped could teach me this very thing: *The Miracle Morning: The Not-So-Obvious Secret Guaranteed to Transform Your Life (Before 8AM)* by Hal Elrod.

"It all begins with accepting total responsibility for every aspect of your life, refusing to blame anyone else and realizing the outer world will always be a reflection of our inner world," Elrod wrote. "Our level of success is always going to parallel our level of personal development. Until we dedicate time each day to developing ourselves into the person we need to be to create the life we want, success is always going to be a struggle to attain."

There were two life-changing lessons for me:

Lesson 1: You can get a good night's sleep, even if you just slept four hours. Elrod said it didn't matter whether he slept four, five, six, seven or more hours, he was always going to get a good night's sleep if he told himself he'd wake up feeling great. If he said he was going to feel tired and groggy, he would.

I wasn't sure I believed it, so I tried it one night. I had a networking meeting at 6 a.m., but it was after midnight before I crawled into bed. I took a big breath, smiled and said, "OK, Athena! You are going to wake up feeling refreshed and five hours is plenty of sleep!"

I woke up feeling amazing.

Lesson 2: I needed an actionable morning routine. Elrod's actionable framework was called Life S.A.V.E.R.S and stands for Silence, Affirmations, Visualization, Exercise, Reading and Scribing.

I wasn't ready for exercise. And if I was really going to get serious about doing this every day without fail, it needed to include things I was really going to do. Since I was already reading so many books and reading was already part of every day, I changed that to talking to God.

My list became this:

1. Wake up early.
2. Clean for 10 minutes.
3. Talk to God.
4. Affirmations.
5. Meditate for 10 minutes.
6. Visualization.
7. Write for 10 minutes.
8. Set my most important tasks for the day.

I was confident I could complete this list every day. I showed the list to Jamie, and we both agreed to start here. This was going to be a piece of cake! I was already working on annual goal books. And even though I hadn't accomplished any large goals, I was pretty solid on the routine of doing daily grateful exercises.

I surprised myself when I added talking to God to my list. I had been going to church for about a year and deeply committed to learning more about God and learning more from scripture. I enjoyed going to church and it seemed the lessons were so valuable. But now, I was committing to growing in that daily relationship with Him.

In the summer of 2014, I accepted my Lord Jesus Christ as my savior, and I got baptized. I was previously baptized as an 8-year-old child but not because I actually believed or had any part in the decision making. This time I wanted to do it because it was my choice. My decision.

There was a part of me that really wanted to believe all of my sins were forgiven, but not only that, when I went under the water, that it would be a burial of my old life. My old life would be wiped away, it would be gone. I knew that choosing to walk with God was going to continue to help me heal. Did I understand when I went into the water what true surrender really was? Not at all.

"And this is life eternal, that they might know thee the only true God, and Jesus Christ, whom thou hast sent" -- John 17:3.

The newly formed list seemed easy enough. All I had to do was wake up, complete the list and go about my day. Except execution — especially when I first started — was laughable.

Waking up early was easy enough. I had always been an early bird, so the 5 a.m. alarm clock never bothered me. Secondly, I had always kept my house fairly tidy, so cleaning for 10 minutes every morning was always fairly simple to implement.

Talking to God. Well, this took some work.

My conversations with God would begin right after my cleaning was done. I would grab a big cup of steamy coffee, plop down in the chair next to the back door, light up a cherry cigar — yes, I smoked — and begin my conversation.

"OK, God, here I am. Hello, are you there?"

He never answered, but I would start by telling him about my day, discuss whatever I was having trouble with and then thank him. I am not quite sure I believed that He was listening, but I did it anyway. Every morning with my coffee.

Meditation wasn't easy either. I had never meditated before, so naturally, I wasn't even sure what I was supposed to do. I would start by sitting up straight in my big, green, comfy living room chair, close my eyes and try to keep my mind quiet. It never worked. Within a few moments the chatter would begin.

"Did I take the dog out? He probably needs to go potty. I should make another pot of coffee. Oh, I hope they have more of that eggnog coffee down at Fresh Thyme. I sure love that stuff. Too bad it's only seasonal. Speaking of Fresh Thyme, I need to do some grocery shopping. I am out of eggs. Eggs. I loved poached eggs. I need to learn how to cook eggs better. My hard-boiled eggs are always gray. How do I get them bright yellow?"

My judgy brain always tried to take over. One time, I was determined. I am going to keep my mind quiet! Quiet! I was on a roll for the first two minutes. Every time a thought would enter my head, I would quickly push it out. The next thing I know, my friend Dennis is tapping my hand. "Hey, didn't you have someplace to be at 9:30?" Oh, for criminy sake, I had fallen asleep. Day after day, every time I tried to meditate I would fall asleep. After weeks and weeks of failed attempts at 10 minutes, I dropped it down to five and started taking guided meditation classes to teach me how to quiet the mind. Many of those early guided meditations were focused on paying attention to the breath. Breathe in. Now breathe out. Breathe in one, two, three, four. Now, breathe out. It took several months, but I finally got to a point where I could keep every thought out of my head for five minutes and pay attention only to my breath. A mindfulness practice taught me how to be still and to listen.

"Your speaking is the first effect of your thinking. Every word you speak creates a ripple throughout the entire universe. Your speaking influences your actions, and over time and with repetitions, your actions shape the person you become." -- Greg Amundson

Affirmations were a challenge. I didn't know what affirmations to write, but I came up with five that I said in the mirror every morning:

1. I love the person I am becoming.
2. I deserve to be happy and successful.
3. I let go of the negative feelings about myself and accept all that is good.
4. I am worthy of all the good things that happen in my life.
5. I am smart, I am capable, and I am beautiful.

Did I believe them? No. But I said them out loud despite those feelings. My only hope was one day I would believe them.

Writing for 10 minutes: Initially, I would just sit and scribble thoughts for 10 minutes. But it was just mindless writing. I had a problem figuring out what I should be writing about. If I was going to spend 10 minutes doing this every day, certainly it should be meaningful.

My daily reading had exposed me to yet another book I believed could solved my mindless writing conundrum. The book was 365 Thank Yous: The Year a Simple Act of Daily Gratitude Changed My Life by John Kra-lik. The book was a perfect illustration of how simple acts of gratitude can lead to better things. Even though things in my life weren't perfect, perhaps in my quest to simply feel better, I could express being grateful for all of the things I already had. I loved the idea. Instead of just writing scribbles, I would take that time to write 10 things I was grateful for and send someone a thank you card every day.

The list evolved. I would add and subtract things, change the time on certain activities. After months of practice, I got to a point where it just became second nature. I would wake up and not even think about what I would do that first hour; it was pretty solidified. After six months of looking in the mirror and saying an affirmation, I would let it go and add a new one.

I made a valiant effort to look at the goal book more often throughout the year when I realized that tossing it into the corner wasn't really working that well. I started putting events on my calendar to remind me quarterly to set time for a goal book review and also incorporated ritual days. These are specific things that you do once a week. I discovered by year-end that even the quarterly check-ins weren't working out that well. I would look at the goal books and constantly tell myself, "Crap, I was going to do that this quarter, wasn't I?"

Months went by and my daily habits were consistent, my weekly ritual days were solid and I was forcing myself to look at my goal book once a month. It took setting reminders and alarms so I would physically have to drag the book out and look at it. Life seemed routine until one day I got a phone call that changed how I looked at things.

★　★　★

The call came late at night in the fall of 2015.

My stepbrother Colin had passed away. Colin was Shelly's middle son and was five days older than me. He had overdosed on his prescription medicine. For years, he had mental problems: bipolar, manic and schizophrenic episodes. He had been checked into mental institutions many times. I wasn't very close to him, but I can't tell you how many times I wondered if

I could have helped him more. Was he screaming for help, and I couldn't hear him? I didn't even know where he was for 10 years, but I thought of him often. It haunted me. And now he was dead.

The guilt I felt for not being there was horrible. My legs were in such terrible condition that I feared getting on the plane to attend his funeral.

And then one night, I was lying in bed almost asleep. My mind was just wandering in its endless abyss. I was thinking about Colin's mental problems and his death. All of a sudden, I jumped out of bed and started pounding on my laptop. OK, I didn't really jump. I just moved quicker than usual.

I spent six hours researching bipolar, read articles on manic episodes and schizophrenic episodes. How had I not made this connection before?

"Many individuals with bipolar disorder have relatives with other mood, anxiety, and psychotic disorders (such as depression or schizophrenia)," according to the U.S. National Library of Medicine.

I researched Colin's known mental issues, and for the first time in my life, I asked, "Are they genetic? Where did he get them from?"

Some of the articles confirmed a possible genetic connection. Had he received them from Shelly? Is there the slightest possibility she had undiagnosed mental disorders that would explain her erratic behavior?

My mouth hit the floor. Shelly could be seemingly normal sometimes. To the outside world she could seem sweet and perfectly loving. But there were other times when she could go from angel to the warrior of death in two and two-tenth seconds. Her behavior was not normal. The way this woman could go into screaming fits in a half second and then be fine several minutes later was not normal. The way this woman could beat a helpless child and smile and laugh through it was not normal. Obviously, she was gone, so there was no way for me to confirm this. However, it was the first time in my life that my childhood started to make sense to me. Her son had mental disorders that eventually killed him. Who's to say some of these mental disorders were not genetic? If this were true, then I just had the first logical explanation for my childhood. It made perfect sense.

I took my ah-ha moment to Jamie. She listened intently and rocked back and forth in her chair.

There was at least a minute or two of silence.

"Athena, hypothetically, if this were true — now, let's say this is the case. How would you feel about her and your life knowing this? Does it change how you feel?"

I started crying.

"Yeah, actually it does."

"Tell me how."

"If this were true, then perhaps she didn't even know she had bipolar disorder. She clearly had been depressed for a long time, which is a side effect of bipolar."

"How do you know she was depressed?"

Tears were rolling down my face.

"Because I think she committed suicide, too."

"What?"

Jamie was shocked.

"Yes. One of my family members told me that everyone thought she died from diabetes but the morning they found her Brad also found a note. Brad hid it from the medical providers and told those who were present never to share it with anyone. Shelly had been sick and in the hospital so many times, the fact that she died never alarmed anyone. Apparently, she overdosed on insulin. That's all I know."

Jamie was speechless.

"Why did you never tell me that?"

"Because whether her kidneys failed from an insulin overdose or they failed because her body just finally gave out didn't matter too much. Everyone always knew her body wouldn't last forever. I wasn't there, so I can't confirm if it was true or not, but now it makes perfect sense. She wasn't right, Jamie. She just wasn't right. She had thoughts she couldn't control, she had problems in her body she couldn't control, and I was simply collateral damage. It had nothing to do with me, and, quite frankly, I feel bad for her. I am not saying it was right, but I am saying I understand."

"What are you saying? You can put yourself in her shoes?"

I sat in the chair speechless for several minutes.

"Yeah. Yeah, I guess I can. I want to let it go. I don't want to carry this anymore.

I cried a lot that night. Not because of the weight that had lifted from my shoulders, but because I felt like I had an entirely different perspective when it came to Shelly's surviving boys.

Admittedly, we weren't close growing up. We weren't even that close as adults. I am sure much of the reason started when we were kids. Her three boys were treated so much differently than us, and unfortunately, years of favoritism had caused a great deal of animosity — at least with me.

As an adult, I would roll my eyes every time I saw one of her boys post a Facebook tribute on Mother's Day or some other holiday, telling the world how amazing and wonderful she was. And then I would have to read the slew of comments from Shelly's friends and family, remembering her as this precious gift to the world.

"Oh, your mother was the sweetest, most amazing human."

It used to make my skin crawl. I would get so mad when I saw these.

But that night, I saw things differently. I saw grown men who had lost their mother in their teens. A mother that loved them dearly. To them, she really was a good mom. There was almost an instant sense of relief that they had never been hit the way I had been hit and abused so severely. Why would I want that for them? Was it their fault? No. Not at all. Why on Earth would I want any memory of a mother for either of them to be bad? I felt an empathy that had not previously been there. I respected the fact she was a different memory for them.

★　★　★

I was feeling mentally stronger. But I had to do something about my weight. I didn't want to die.

"Athena, it's serious. You need to get pressure off these legs now," my orthopedic surgeon told me in December 2015.

Why had I not been making improvements with my weight? Mentally I felt stronger than ever. What was wrong with me?

By the end of 2015, I realized that other than writing down my goals, I wasn't sure what the hell I was supposed to do. I was getting really good at incorporating daily habits, but I was not moving any mountains in terms of my weight. I was convinced these goal books didn't work, so in December when I was usually buying the "new year of goals" book, I opted out.

I still hadn't lost any weight. These goal books don't work.

## JOURNAL ENTRY JAN. 3, 2016

*The bone on bone on my right side caused issues for so long it was starting to affect the left side in horrible fashion, and it required steroid injections every 4 months. The medicine wears off at about two and a half months, and I live on daily hydrocodone pills until the next injection date. The pills make me tired, irritable…and walking around over the last three months on walking canes makes it difficult to go anywhere. Shopping and meeting clients take every bit of energy that I have. The idea of having to go grocery shopping can literally bring tears to my eyes. I wish I could swallow my pride and ride around in one of those carts at the store, but I can't. So, I walk down the aisles and grit my teeth…keeping my head down so they can't see my eyes welling. All I feel most days is pounding in my knees. They see a fat person at the store. I have become a bit of a hermit, I will admit. I hate people staring at me.*

*Every doctor out there will tell you that to lose weight you have to work out. Work out….That phrase became something I hated. I don't use that word in my vocabulary normally because it's such a strong word. "Hate." I HATE working out. It hurts just to walk around my house. It actually hurts just thinking about doing any kind of working out. And that fear of pain in my legs that I knew would happen if I started moving kept me from doing it. I have been through a lot of pain in my life, and the self-inflicted pain isn't an option.*

★   ★   ★

I didn't like the idea but reluctantly promised my medical team I would look into bariatric surgery. It was the most hopeless feeling I had ever had.

# LESSON 12

*I believe one of the reasons it took me so long to forgive was because I was secretly keeping score. I wanted to get even. We are naturally protective beings, especially when we feel threatened, so it's logical that we would want to retaliate when attacked. Revenge is attractive.*

*Holding on to this desire for revenge for so long wasn't necessarily unusual, but the problem was that this desire took on a life of its own. It kept me anchored to my past. I got sucked in and couldn't figure out how to get out.*

*Holding on to this desire for revenge meant that I was living in a state of anger almost constantly. I didn't know it and it wasn't conscious, but it was there. Because it was present, it was manifesting other conditions like depression, stress and anxiety. Pretty soon I was looking for ways to cope — and we wonder how the cycle of self-destruction perpetuates.*

*Forgiveness gave me the opportunity to set down the burden of revenge.*

# CHAPTER 13:
## SURRENDER AND MIRACLES

I went to visit my folks in Texas at Christmastime shortly after Colin passed away in 2015.

Two weeks later while I was on my drive back to Minnesota and my legs were killing me. After about every 15 minutes or so, I had to change the position of my legs — especially the right one. I would have to stretch them out, move them back in, turn them to the right or left or otherwise wiggle them so my knees wouldn't lock up. I couldn't take pain pills on the road because they made me drowsy.

By the time I got to northern Iowa, I just couldn't go on. I was in so much pain, I was crying while trying to drive in the middle of a blizzard. I couldn't see anything. By the time I pulled up to the motel, I didn't think I would make it to the front door. My legs just stopped working. They wouldn't move. I couldn't feel them anymore. Every step I took felt like knives were driving into my kneecaps. They were so stiff I had to grab both pant legs with my hands and literally pull them forward — right foot, left foot until I made it to the check-in desk.

The horrible pain on the drive caused my whole body to stiffen to a point where I couldn't even turn my head properly. I sat on the toilet in the motel room that night bawling my eyes out because I couldn't even move to properly wipe myself. I had to strip down and take a shower because I couldn't get my hand far enough back.

After I got home, I attended the first informational meeting required in the bariatric process. I couldn't take it anymore. Something needed to change. It took a while to accept this new path. I had fought it my whole life, had utter disdain for it, and here I was going through the motions and the process so I could get insurance approval and a green light to proceed. In my heart, it's not what I wanted, but at the time, I felt like I lacked options. I couldn't see any other way to get the weight off my legs as quickly and urgently as the doctors were saying was necessary.

My heart and brain felt stronger than ever at this point in my life, but there was still one issue I had been unable to deal with: my weight. All the years of therapy had done amazing things to help my heart heal and to feel better. But throughout therapy, I was still eating and gaining weight. Something was still there.

A month later, I started a new book, "The Grief Recovery Handbook," by John W. James. It's a five-step recovery program for those experiencing the confusion, isolation and loneliness caused by emotional loss. My and Jamie's goals were to continue deep diving into the negative experiences that caused the weight gain in the first place and to address the issue of health loss. There was clearly so much emotional pain surrounding the topic of weight and food that Jamie and I hadn't previously been able to address. My relationship with food was formed so many years ago that chiseling down those false truths about my body and food was necessary. I had walked a very convoluted path to discover how to grieve my weight gains and deal with teasing, torment and comments in my past. I always said I was fine. But bottom line: It wasn't fine. I couldn't even go to the grocery store without getting dirty looks, and every day the hurt just got worse.

My past triggered my eating. Eating caused weight gain. Weight gain caused grief. I wasn't dealing with my grief, so I ate to soothe my pain.

There are many myths about grief. These myths make the ability to grieve impossible. Common myths according to John James:

1.  Don't feel bad. Just let it go. Don't wallow in it.

2.  Replace the loss. Get a new guy, get a dog.

3.  Grieve alone. Don't let anyone see you cry. I will give you something to cry about. If you are going to cry, go to your room.

4.  Just give it time. Just wait. Time will heal all wounds.

5.  Be strong for others. You are not important. Always put others first.

6.  Keep busy. Distractions are always a good idea. Keep working and try to just forget about it.

I spent my life stuffing my face when I was angry or hurting instead of doing what I should have been doing: grieving. Because of this, a certain kind of crud built up around my heart that just seemed to thicken every year.

"Grief is negative and cumulatively negative," James explained.

For me personally, every time something in my life happened that caused me trauma of any kind, I didn't realize it, and it triggered all of those past hurts I had never dealt with. My heart broke. And because my heart had built up all this crap around it, I couldn't see it, and it would cause yet another downward spiral. For me, it always meant eating and more and more weight gain. Ultimately, the answer for me was to replace my method of grieving. I needed to learn how to find different coping mechanisms instead of food. Food was all I knew.

"OK, so how do I find different coping mechanisms? I don't do this shit on purpose! This is all I know!"

"Athena, you use food to cope," Jamie said. "You must find another way to get through life's struggles. Everyone has struggles, but you deal with them in a very self-destructive way. It started before you were even old enough to understand. That wasn't your fault. However, you need to recognize this has to change. If you decide to get surgery, what's going to happen after surgery if you can't get this under control? You will go right back to where you started. You use food, and whether you realize it or not, it's a direct reflection of how you feel about yourself. You need to keep working on those affirmations. You need to believe them! Henry Emmons — have you ever heard of him?"

"No, who's that?"

"He wrote a book. OK, so he says that your brain right now has been created as a direct response to the life you have led up to this point. Let me give you an example. Think of your life as a pasture. You are the farmer. Every day you wake up, you walk outside, and you take a path to a clearing in the pasture. Every night, you return. Over the years, this habit created a visible path. Because you wake up and take that same path, it's easier to stay on that path because it's what you know. However, there's nothing saying you can't carve a new path. Just because food is all you know doesn't mean you can't replace it with something else. You are going to have to rewire the brain and create a new path."

"I understand what you are saying, but I don't know how to do that."

"You are going to have to find what works for you."

Did I understand what she was saying? Yes, absolutely. But did I understand how to correct all of the negative wiring in my head? No.

I made a declaration that every time I felt the urge to eat, I would start reading or talking to God. Whatever I was thinking about, I was creating. So, I needed to flush my head with other things. I didn't know if it was going to work, but I began. I started reading every spiritual or self-help book I could get my hands on. I was already a fan of many of the topics: the Law of Attraction, karma principles, decluttering life. Reading became an enjoyment. The more I read, the easier it got. Some of those books are:

*The Power of Now* by Eckhart Tolle,

*The Secret* by Rhonda Byrne,

*The 5 Love Languages* by Gary Chapman,

*The Art of Happiness* by Dalai Lama XIV,

*The Seven Spiritual Laws of Success* by Deepak Chopra,

*Big Magic* by Elizabeth Gilbert,

*The Life-Changing Magic of Tidying Up* by Marie Kondo,

*The Subtle Art of Not Giving a F\*ck* by Mark Manson,

*You Are a Badass* by Jen Sincero,

*The Happiness Project* by Gretchen Rubin.

So many months and so many books. I was even working in goal books again, trying to learn how to set realistic goals. When I wasn't working, reading or spending time on my goal books, I was sitting at the back door with my cup of coffee talking to God. I constantly asked for guidance regarding the surgery and help making the right decisions.

In April, I had my first breakthrough. I started working on fears and emotional attachments when it came to how I felt about my body. The weight was clearly some kind of attachment for me. One that I was very fearful of letting go. I started with something simple: my hair.

Pretty silly, huh?

I always had long hair. I am not sure why, other than I always received compliments on my hair. I felt like if I cut it off, I would have nothing. I had convinced myself that it was the only beautiful feature I had. If it were cut, my beauty would be gone. I didn't feel beautiful, so what's the difference?

It took me a couple of weeks, but I remember sitting in that stylist's chair thinking, "What the hell are you doing?" I had to work through this idea that my hair was somehow connected to what makes me beautiful. It was hard, but I embraced the change. In fact, when it was all off I could not believe how good my head felt. I loved that it only took 20 minutes to blow dry and style, and I could be ready much quicker. Who knew I would like it more? Honestly, It was a weird sense of freedom.

The next several months were a constant state of waiting. I essentially put my life on hold while I waited for surgery. I didn't want to make any long-term plans. I was always waiting for the next doctor's appointment, waiting for the next weigh-in and secretly fighting the process at every turn. I consistently delayed appointments on purpose. I had insurance approval for months. All I had to do was set a date. I hadn't done it. I continued to eat and didn't care about losing any weight. Why bother?

By October 2016, my legs hurt so badly I was on 24-hour pain medication — specifically, hydrocodone. I was popping anywhere from two to four pills a day — sometimes more — to deal with the constant throbbing and pain. My legs couldn't hold my weight anymore, and I was on two walking canes. I didn't leave my house very often because of how difficult it became to move around. I started suffering from mysterious symptoms: severe edema, blackouts, losing feeling in my arms and hands, feeling like my heart was beating a mile a minute and memory problems. It seemed like I was always getting horrible sores on the insides of my legs that were filled with pus — most likely from poor hygiene. My indigestion and heartburn were so bad I had acid coming up my throat at night. I had hemorrhoids that were so bad that every time I went to the bathroom, I cried. I tried every remedy for them, but nothing worked. Bathing became exhausting. It would take over an hour to take a simple shower. I just didn't have the energy anymore, so most days I didn't even try. It wouldn't be uncommon for me to stay in the same outfit for days at a time. Because of this, I had a horrible odor. I didn't want to go to the store, I didn't want to go anywhere. It got so bad I didn't want anyone to see the condition I was in.

I finally made the decision to have surgery. I didn't know from one day to the next if my legs were going to give out. I was taking so many pain pills I knew I couldn't go on like this. I had no fight left. I only remember leaving my home once or twice during the month of December. I went to a baby shower for a friend, but the outing was so exhausting I vowed I wouldn't do it again because I spent the entire next day sleeping. I was so exhausted.

My bariatric surgery was scheduled for January 11, 2017. My body was giving out. I didn't know how to attack over 300 pounds of weight I needed to lose. It was impossible without surgery.

★　★　★

Normally during Christmas, I would visit my parents in Texas, but they decided to head out to the West Coast to visit my siblings and their kids. They asked if I wanted to go; I declined. There was no way I could think about going. I could purchase a first-class ticket and I might be OK with my seat, but I couldn't even fathom how I was going to get from my car down to the terminal. There was no way my legs could get me that far. I got too large to travel, so I knew I would be spending Christmas alone for the first time in my life.

The thought of spending the holidays alone in my now-prison sent me down an eating spiral once again. I was so sad and so lonely. The last weight on the scale recorded was 449.5. When I weighed myself after that, the scale blinked "error." I was somewhere near 500 pounds, but the exact number I will never know.

Christmas morning came. It felt like any ordinary day. I didn't want to shower. I just laid on the couch. I tried to enjoy the family festivities via Skype, but had to keep putting the monitor down so they wouldn't see me cry. I had to just say my goodbyes because I couldn't handle watching them laugh and have a good time. I cried in my chair and tried to watch TV. I played on my phone, held my dogs. What else could I do? I wondered how many hydrocodones it would take to make it all go away.

I got bored Christmas evening and started trolling social media and You-Tube. I came across an abundance of testimonials regarding weight loss surgery. I sat there for hours and hours listening to horror stories about people who had the surgery and wished they hadn't done it. Some of them carried scars, massive amounts of loose skin, and told stories of having to have the surgery twice! I saw people who had lost hundreds of pounds, only to gain the weight right back.

What was I doing? I was terrified. There was a voice in the back of my mind that kept saying, "Don't do it. Don't do it." I heard it loud and clear, but with that came sadness and sorrow and darkness I struggle to describe. I knew I could face severe complications, even death. But without it, I could still die. I had no clear option other than surgery. I had nothing to fall back on. I was desperate and on the brink of swallowing the entire bottle of hydrocodones in the kitchen.

I was lying on the couch and burst into horrible sobbing. I had never cried this way in my life. I was screaming and crying. My sobbing turned to rage. I was so angry. I cried out to God.

"God, how could you do this to me? I have tried to trust you. I have begged for years for help to get this weight off and still nothing! Haven't I gone through enough pain? Haven't I bled enough? Why weren't you ever there for me? Why does it always feel like every time I need you the most, you aren't there? But here I am trying and struggling to believe! Why?"

It wasn't one of my prouder moments. I was screaming obscenities at God. I just wanted to die. Why was I the one who had to experience so much pain and heartache and trauma? Why was I the one who had to endure years of physical and verbal torture from other people — things I had to carry with me my whole life? I just didn't understand. I understood nothing.

"I am asking for your help. Please help me. I don't know how to get this weight off; I don't know how to climb this mountain. I don't have the tools without surgery. I don't know how! Please, God. Help me, please. I know you can help, God. I beg you. Please be there for me now."

I cried out to God for hours before falling asleep in the middle of my living room floor. I didn't even have the strength to get up.

It was dark. I couldn't see anything.

I felt like I was somewhere between deep sleep and half-consciousness.

I didn't have any feeling left in my body. I couldn't move my arms or my legs. "This is it," I thought. My legs finally gave out.

I heard a voice.

"Athena, I heard every word spoken. I have always been here."

"What do you mean you have always been here. No, you haven't."

"Haven't I answered every prayer?"

"How have you answered every prayer?" I screamed.

"I was there when you were young. You asked for a dad. That dad has loved you since the day he met you. You prayed that you would grow up strong. You did. Are you not strong, Athena? I heard you when you asked for help.

That woman has walked with you for many years helping you and guiding you. I heard your prayer for the flowers, Athena. Can you smell the flowers? You live in Minnesota, Athena. The help you asked for a very long time ago is right here. Right now."

"What help did I ask for a very long time ago?"

"You prayed that you could finish what you started. I heard you. But Athena, there was much for you to learn."

And then the voice was gone. My eyes were now wide open. I stared at the ceiling. Did that just happen again, or did I dream that whole thing?

I was confused.

Can I smell the flowers? Can I smell the flowers? What in the hell did that mean?

Initially, I shrugged it off. What a weird dream! I could smell my body odor, so I knew it was time for me to take a shower. An hour later, I was back in the living room watching TV. I stumbled onto QVC and found myself watching "Deal of the Day" — beautiful hydrangeas in 6-inch pots.

The coffee cup I was holding dropped onto my wooden floors and shattered. I was shaking. I don't remember being more freaked out in my life.

★   ★   ★

Nick and I used to travel extensively to the East Coast.

One of my favorite places in the whole world is Nantucket. We went during the peak of summertime one year. I loved the smell of the ocean air and the sweet blue hydrangea that covered the island.

In 2009, when our relationship was falling apart and I knew I wanted out, I found myself praying to God one hopeless night in our bedroom. I asked for help to make the right decision. I wanted to get the rest of my weight off. I was tired of carrying it around. I needed help. I wanted to finish school and get my graduate degree. I remember a lot of things about that prayer but there was one detail that seemed like a silly request: I wanted my own home that felt safe. I wanted it to look like an East Coast Cape Cod or farmhouse — the ones I loved so much when I visited Nantucket. And I prayed for blue hydrangea.

When I decided to move to Minnesota, I had flown up to visit a couple of times. I was getting frustrated because I couldn't seem to find what I was looking for. I knew I would know it when I saw it. After two visits and seeing nearly 30 homes, the realtor called.

"Athena, I know you are tired, but I have one more for you to see. I think this is the one."

I was so exhausted I didn't want to look at any more houses. But I agreed.

When I pulled up to the front of the house, I knew it. It was the one I had been waiting for.

It was a big red farmhouse. I couldn't see any of the landscaping because it was the middle of winter, but the home couldn't have been any more created just for me. I made an offer that evening and they accepted.

That spring, when the snow melted off, I saw I had various bushes around the house. I had no idea what they were as they were not in bloom. I watched patiently as they grew from wintered brown stalks to these lovely plants with big leaves and then bulbs. When they finally bloomed, I had them: blue hydrangea.

★   ★   ★

My mind started racing trying to understand the other pieces of the message I had heard that night on the living room floor.

I was in Minnesota because "the help you asked for a very long time ago is right here. Right now."

I was on the brink of suicide that night when I prayed in my bedroom back in 2009. The following day, I met my closest friend, Dennis, who happened to live in Minnesota. I bought my home in Minnesota and quickly found Jamie, who had been the one to lead me down this path of healing and recovery. Is this what he meant? Could this possibly be what he was saying?

I thought the fact Dennis was in Minnesota was random. I thought meeting Jamie was also just random. My farmhouse, the blue hydrangea. Was it not?

I hadn't finished what I started, though. I was still heavy. The heaviest I had been in my life. I had not finished what I started.

Now I am a teary-eyed mess. I had a dream very similar to this several years back when the voice was telling me about my dad, and here he was again!

"God, it's me, Athena. Are you still there? I think I heard you. Was that you? God, I haven't finished what I started. I don't know how. Please show me how. I will listen and do whatever you want me to do. I will listen! God, please don't leave. I will do whatever you tell me. I am going to finish what I started, but I need the tools. I need help. Please."

I spent hours that night sitting with my cup of coffee by the back door where I always sat. I shared with God my dreams for the future. I was at a point where I was at the bottom. Giving my problems and desires and wishes for my life to God was all I had left. I still so desperately wanted to believe that everything I experienced wasn't in vain. There was a reason, there was some grand purpose behind all of it. I wanted to believe that everything I just saw was real, somehow.

I was 39 years old. Yes, I had fears I might have waited too long, but still, I prayed for a happy-ever-after with someone and a family of my own.

I prayed to feel better. I prayed to God to please help me walk again.

I prayed for friends.

I prayed for healthy ways to deal with emotional eating.

Although I liked what I did for a living, it didn't inspire me. I wanted to feel inspired, I wanted to inspire others. I didn't know how but I asked.

I prayed to feel happy. I don't know if a feeling of true joy was something I had ever felt. There were happy times but true joy? I didn't know what that felt like.

I prayed for God to please help me finish what I started and be able to attack this weight problem successfully. I prayed for him to make me strong. I needed to be stronger than I ever had been in my life.

It was a lofty list. But, one by one, I gave them to God. I didn't know what it was going to look like or feel like. But I believed.

I am not sure what happened. But I had a sense of peace, of calm. I knew I had just seen and heard something pretty incredible. The thought I was going crazy did cross my mind, but I believed it was some kind of miracle. It did something to my heart because somehow, out of nowhere, I believed that everything I asked for was possible.

# LESSON 13

*By Athena Perez with Sara Krych*

*The moment of true surrender is not when life is over. It's when life truly begins. "Job never saw why he suffered, but he saw God, and that was enough" -- Tim Keller*

*It's natural for us to fear "surrender." After all, surrender in battle means hope is gone, and victory is lost. But surrender to God means we surrender to the One who sees all, knows all and is the giver of all good things. To cling to our burdens is to prefer making mud pies in the slum when we could enjoy a "holiday at the sea." -- C.S. Lewis, The Weight of Glory*

*It's effortless for us to say, God, what do I do? But He tells us in Philippians 4:6, "Do not be anxious about anything, but in every situation, by prayer and petition, with thanksgiving, present your requests to God." We don't need to worry about the how. We just need to believe that He hears and is faithful to complete the work He began (Philippians 1:6). Do we think our struggles are more significant than God? If we do, how small is our God? What would that be saying of Him?*

# CHAPTER 14:
## *THE FIRST 90 DAYS*

That night, I was exhausted.

I had spent 24 hours talking to God, and I was drifting aimlessly in and out of consciousness. The following night there was another dream but this time it was different.

There was no one talking — only scenes and pictures. The first thing I remember seeing was a guy named Mike. I knew this guy from networking meetings. I would call him a friend but more of a business acquaintance. I didn't know him that well, and he played no significant role in my life. We didn't hang out or anything like that, but there he was. Also, in this dream was a gym. I didn't recognize the gym itself partly because I didn't understand where all the equipment was. There were no treadmills or big weight machines you would typically find in a normal gym. I could see people doing activities but nothing like I had known before.

I laughed as soon as I woke up because seeing Mike in my dream seemed so silly to me. I knew he went to a gym only because I had seen him get tagged in social media pictures quite often by a personal trainer friend of his.

I laughed it off because it really was that stupid to me at the time. But on the third night, it happened again. It was Mike, the gym, and this time there was a girl. I didn't recognize her. She had blond hair. I got vibes that somehow she might have been shy, but other than that, I didn't know her.

Once again I woke up thinking how strange it was, but this time I remember feeling odd. Having so many dreams like this was crazy. Was I really losing it?

The fourth night, it happened again. This time, the dream had Mike, the gym, the blond-haired girl and now there was me. Sort of. It was me but I didn't recognize myself. I could tell it was me because of my face, but my eyes looked different. I could tell I was smaller. In one scene I am talking to a group of people. In another scene, I am holding sand in my hands, laughing and talking.

It happened on a fifth and sixth night as well. Every night it was the same thing. But every subsequent night, new elements appeared. A new person or a scene. On New Year's morning, after this had been happening for nearly a week, I finally broke down. I felt with every fiber of my body that God was showing me something, but I didn't know what.

It felt good, it felt peaceful. The only confusion I felt at the time was what these dreams meant. Why did he keep showing me this guy? Why did I keep seeing this gym? Who was the girl? Why don't I recognize myself? I had no doubt that everything was real, and I was meant to take action somehow, but I didn't exactly know what.

On the morning of Monday, January 2 — Day seven of the dreams — I awoke with a feeling of knowing. I felt determined. I was going to listen to every prompt I got. I was going to learn to trust my inner voices as the Holy Spirit and let them guide me. I felt like I had clarity for my mission, and I knew what I needed to do to start feeling better.

The first thing I did was empty my refrigerator. Everything had to go. If it wasn't meat and vegetables, nuts and seeds, fruits, good starches, beans or eggs, I wasn't going to be eating it anymore. That same morning, I called my doctors and let them know I changed my mind about having bariatric surgery. It wasn't a positive reception.

"Athena, I hope you are making the right decision. Without surgery, there is doubt you will successfully get relief on those legs."

"You know what? I am making the right decision."

Click. That was easy.

Next, I sat down with my brand new 2017 goals book and I was going to take the next couple of days to get it all filled out. I knew my mind and actions were powerful. I was going to allow them to create a new life. A new, powerful life. I came to questions regarding goals for specific months. I sat there tapping my head with my pencil. I must have dozed off. I awoke to hear someone laughing. It was laughter I recognized right away, but I was confused because this man had passed away when I was 21. It was my grandpa.

"Haaa haaaaa haaa. Turn around, Athena. Let me take a look at ya." He always said that when I got on the phone with him, and I would laugh and spin around in the kitchen with the phone in my hand. It was confirmation it really was him.

"Athena, I am proud of you. Do you remember that conversation we had when you were just a girl? Do you remember, Athena? Take it one day at a time. Remember what I told you? Take everything you learned and apply it. You already know what to do."

My grandfather was an incredible man. He stopped drinking when he and my grandmother adopted my mom when she was 12. He had a medallion from Alcoholics Anonymous he carried with him. It had gems for every year sober, along with prettier ones for the milestone years. Shortly before his death, he celebrated 50 years sober.

I had a conversation with him one summer when I was 12 as we were out in the backyard sitting next to this big row of lilac bushes. I asked him how he quit drinking.

"I never thought about tomorrow. It was too overwhelming. If I would start thinking about a week or a month from now, it would become too much. So, I didn't. I just woke up in the morning and said, 'Owen, can you stay on your plan today? Yes, I can do it one day.' Today turned into a week, then a month, then a year. I just kept doing it over and over again."

And then he was gone. He was either gone or I woke up. To be honest, I don't know which. I hadn't thought about what my grandpa had said since the day he said it. But it was so real.

I had an epiphany.

I figured out where I kept going wrong in my previous goal books. My goals in previous years weren't reasonable because I kept putting time on them. For instance, some of my goals would look like this: "By June 30, I will be down 50 pounds." Every time I would set a time constraint on one of my goals, it just ended up being a constant series of let-downs, and then I would proceed to beat myself up. I wasn't going to do that anymore. I didn't control time, and I couldn't control speed. This was going to take however long it takes. It might be a year or two or five. I didn't know, but making peace with time was the first thing I did.

Once again, I truly believed God had a hand in replaying that conversation with grandpa. I needed it at that precise moment. For me, it was further confirmation I was making the right decisions. That there had been a mighty intervention I couldn't explain.

I had zero clue what I was doing when I started on Day 1. I knew that whatever I had seen in my dreams was the direction I needed to go. I didn't know what they meant, but I was going to head in that direction. The only discernible thing from the dreams was Mike. Was I supposed to be his friend? Was this the guy God picked for me? Maybe? I didn't know.

I knew God was with me and every time I had a question I had no doubt he was going to help me and point me where I needed to go. I had no doubt. I believed what happened was a miracle and there was simply no doubt God had intervened in my life.

I continued daily reading and writing, but other than my normal daily activities, I didn't want to focus on anything else other than my nutrition for the first 30 days. I had another realization early on in those first two weeks: I shouldn't add too many changes at one time. I can't turn everything upside down all at once or it will all come caving down. I would focus on one thing at a time and then slowly introduce changes. As soon as that change became part of my life, then I would know it was acceptable to introduce something else.

One very profound change happened right away on Day 1. I am not sure how I knew, but there was a prompt for me to "quiet my space."

I knew anything I told myself needed to be positive and come in the form of positive reinforcement. I couldn't afford to tell myself anything negative.

*"Therefore, by disciplining your thinking, you begin to speak a language of positive expectancy."* —Greg Amundson

This required that I also make sure I wasn't hearing anything negative. I couldn't afford outside negativity either. I didn't want to hear anything that was going to upset me. I turned off the TV. No more news, no more politics, no more crime shows, nothing. I would only be able to watch movies that were fun and lighthearted, or I would be able to listen to my music on Pandora. I needed space to think and to talk to God.

I also needed time to work on daily rewiring. All those years of therapy, I was finally starting to understand what this meant. I made a commitment to working on rewiring my brain with the objective of creating a new path one day at a time. When it came to food, I thought about the kinds of things I was going to eat. I decided I was choosing not to use the word "can't." I wasn't going to say, "I can't have this" because I could have whatever I wanted. I wanted to be able to feel like I was in control of my body, not the other way around.

"I can't have this" changed to "I am choosing not to have this, or I don't want it."

This tiny phrase change probably made the biggest impact over the next month. Knowing that if I really wanted to, I could buy a piece of cake and not feel guilty was so powerful because I didn't set limitations on myself. Because I told myself I could have whatever I wanted helped stop the constant barrage of negative self-talk and guilt trips. I didn't have to feel guilty anymore. The power to make a good choice did more for confidence building than anything I had ever done.

By the end of the first month, I was down 26.5 pounds, and the only thing I had done was nutrition changes. I noticed it first in my energy levels. I wasn't taking midday naps. The shaking and lightheadedness were gone. I was sleeping better at night, which paid off in huge ways. I could think clearer, I could focus better, and I wasn't sleeping at 6 p.m. My heartburn and hemorrhoids were also gone. I was still walking with both canes, but walking was getting easier. My Fitbit was recording more daily steps. My mood had improved tenfold. I was smiling.

★   ★   ★

By the end of the second month, my routine was fairly set.

I had "shining habits" and "ritual days." They kept me focused on daily tasks and weekly time for myself.

My daily tasks were the following: Eat healthy, drink 80 ounces of water, write a thank-you card, spend time talking to God, read a daily devotional and study scripture, clean house for 15 minutes, write down 10 things I was grateful for, meditate for five minutes, and set my three most important tasks for the day. I know, it sounds like a lot, but I used to bang through it fairly quickly.

"Ritual days" were the activities I did weekly: Sabbath Sundays, Reading Mondays, Go to Bed Early Tuesdays, Car Wash Wednesdays, Spiritual Thursdays, Shopping Friday and Adventure Saturdays.

When I was getting ready for a networking meeting one morning, I found myself standing in front of my closet staring at "skinnier" clothes and wondering if I would be brave enough to try them on. There was this one pair of jeans in particular that I hadn't worn in over a year, maybe longer. There is nothing special about them other than they are soft, and they have holes in them which are my favorite kind of jeans. I had to put them away over a year ago because I ate myself out of them. But that morning, there I was, holding the hanger half biting my lower lip, wondering if today was the day. Not only was I able to get them on, but they fit like a glove. I thought I was going to start crying. It was an overwhelming feeling. For someone that had been stuck in yoga gear for so long, being able to wear something normal made me feel human again. I felt a smile that hadn't been there in years, and I knew a prayer had been answered. I told God in my prayers that I just wanted to feel better. It had happened. I did feel better. Knowing this only made my faith stronger. I knew what I heard, and I had absolute faith in what I saw in those dreams. I knew more was to come; I just didn't know what.

★   ★   ★

So, who was this guy Mike, and why had he been in my dreams?

It was time to find out. What to do, what to do? I did what any female might have done: I stalked his Facebook profile. Why was this person revealed multiple times? It didn't make any sense, but there was a prompt to "head that way." It's hard to describe the feeling; it just didn't go away.

I must have spent at least an hour reading posts and looking at pictures. I couldn't figure it out, but I did get hung up on a few of the images. Many of them I had seen over the previous year or two. He belonged to a Cross-Fit gym. He got tagged quite often by a trainer. I started looking at that trainer's business page. Something jumped out at me, and I knew I needed to reach out. I wanted to see if perhaps he could help me get moving again. I had never done any kind of real physical activity or sport for most of my life. I had been off my right leg for so long that it was atrophied. I had no other goal at the time but to simply learn to walk and move again. This seemed to be the logical first step.

I met with the trainer, Kevin, about a week later. I was nervous and panicked about training in a CrossFit gym. Gyms for someone my size were typically not safe places, but I agreed to drive down there. I was about 10 miles away, driving down this ridiculously long road to the gym. It felt like 100 miles. My knees were shaking like it was a sub-freezing day in January. What am I doing? I panicked. I was scared. I could feel sweat beading up on my forehead, and I think it was the beginning of an anxiety attack. I sat in the parking lot just trying to calm my breathing so I could work up the courage to walk inside. Scared isn't the right word. I was terrified. Then I heard the voice, "Athena, it's going to be just fine." There was that voice again. But I didn't just hear it this time — I felt peace.

I approached the gym's front door, took a deep breath, counted to three and opened it slowly. There was a young kid at the front desk that greeted me kindly but thankfully there was nobody else there. Had there been people there, I might have run out the door. People don't understand this kind of anxiety, but it's real. I didn't stay long but something about it calmed me down. I wish I could say with certainty what about it made me feel calm. It was just a feeling of knowing I was in the right place. It was a scary moment, but the voice said it would be OK and it was. I faced that fear. It felt empowering. I called Kevin back and told him I would attend the Friday event to which he had invited me. I was hesitant but agreed to do it. The event happened to be the last night of the 2017 Reebok CrossFit Games Open.

The night went far better than I ever expected. So many warm greetings and so many people came up to me to introduce themselves and asked if I was going to be joining the gym.

Two of the people sitting next to me tapped me on the shoulder and said, "Hey! You see that right there? That's going to be you next year...I laughed. That was the silliest thing I had ever heard.

At some point about an hour after I had arrived, I caught a glimpse of a woman sitting in the second row of the crowd, clapping and cheering as the athletes competed. She turned her head, she looked at me and smiled. I smiled back and froze. I recognized her. I didn't know where from, but I knew this girl. I spent most of the night trying to figure it out, but I gave up and almost forgot about it until I was sitting in my car in the parking lot. It was a cold March evening, and I was heating up the car so my poor fingers wouldn't freeze off during the drive home. I suddenly remembered: She was the blond-haired girl in the dream. Just like that, I knew where I had seen her. I burst into tears. How could this be? I took it as a second confirmation that the gym was also the one in the dream and that I was where I needed to be. I knew in my heart I was on the right path.

JOURNAL ENTRY: MARCH 24, 2017

*I walked into that CrossFit Gym tonight I was telling you about. That scared, fearful woman that I became was waiting for someone to stare. I was waiting for them to laugh at me. I found myself looking around the room quite a bit just to get confirmation that I was right. Someone was going to be mean or cruel and it would give me validation that me attending a CrossFit gym was a bad idea. Somebody freaking look at me so I can validate this for myself!\*&$\*$&$ (!!!............. It didn't happen.*

*Here's what did happen. They were so kind and friendly. One by one they would come by and introduce themselves. I had braced myself for the worst — just like I keep doing at these new experiences, and my fears are just that. Fears. For that, there are no words tonight. Only tears. Life is getting better, and it's a bit overwhelming. I prayed for this, and now it's happening, and now I almost don't know what to do with it. It seems so unreal. How could this be?*

*I know that there is a possibility that so much of my paranoia were self-created. I am scared almost every place I go, but it's getting better, and it's getting easier and each experience is changing my life....*

Because I didn't get any dirty looks and because no one was mean to me, it made the decision to train at this location with Kevin twice a week tolerable. I desperately wanted to be able to walk easier. I wanted to walk better. This was all I thought about.

Every day I prayed, "God please give me the strength to go back. I know you are with me."

My first few training sessions were very light in terms of activity. On my first day in the gym, I was still using one cane to stabilize my walking. It was cold and icy outside, so I needed a little extra support. I was extremely limited in what I could do. Kevin and I took all of the body measurements and focused on very simple activities like leg lifts, arm raises and anything that could be done from a lying or seated position. Even simple training sessions twice a week really took it out of me. I was exhausted after every session — like I had just run a marathon. I would go home and sleep for hours. Just learning how to use my arms and legs in very simple movements was challenging. I was so sore and uncomfortable. But every new session I completed inspired me to do another. And then another.

I began seeing more people at the gym because our training session times started varying. Sometimes we would meet at 10 a.m., other times noon. So, I was getting exposed to other members. Before too long, I was calling many of them friends. The joy I felt in people excited to see me kept me coming back. They were nice. They smiled at me. They gave me hugs and high fives. Joy, however, was also shared with daily struggles but profound lessons.

## JOURNAL ENTRY: MARCH 30, 2017

*Discovering life again after being alone and cooped up for so long at times feels like Shawshank (Redemption). There is a conversation that Andy has with Red in the movie. Sometimes I feel it's equivalent to the right and left sides of my brain communicating with one another. One, despite going through the worst, understands… profoundly this concept of Hope. The other… bruised by life, is a bit cynical. I don't know what life in a body I can be proud of feels like, but I can see it. I must have daily conversations with the "Red" part of my brain that says, "You can forget about that, it's futile." To some degree, this is a daily struggle. One side of me is elated, the other side is struggling to catch up. Everything seems new to me and I am learning to live a different life, but with that, I leave comfort zones. Some of them have been challenging because they are…in fact…familiar. Once you get out of what feels "familiar," everything is unknown. Here's a small guide for the terrified — I am learning that in order to be successful — you must get comfortable with discomfort. There really is no other way.*

# LESSON 14

*By Athena Perez with Tasia Percevecz*

---

*Listen to the nudges. The Holy Spirit's voice will be as loud as your willingness to listen.*

*What are these nudges? Many of us don't recognize help when it shows up. A spiritual nudge is more than intuition. It's an answer to a prayer or an invitation to do the work that God is calling us to do: change our own life or the lives He places in our paths.*

*The very tangible and real Holy Spirit is within each of us, nudging us to make a choice or to pay attention to someone or something. How many times have each of us failed to ignore that little voice because we didn't understand what it was when it showed up? Sometimes it's easy to overlook those nudges because we think they are merely passing thoughts or the usual chatter we hear in our heads during a busy day, so those blessings meant for us float away like a balloon.*

*When there is something God is calling us to do, it can start as a feeling: "There is something I need to do." As time goes on, it can become more urgent: "There is something I need to do, and I need to do it right now." You could call it a "lead" or a "prompt," but frequently, it is merely a sense of knowing. It can feel like clarity, it can feel joyful, and sometimes it is instant peace.*

*There are many ways God reveals himself. It can happen through a song that speaks to us, or through worship. It could be the voice in your head that won't be quiet, a message on a billboard. Many times, it will be a message you keep seeing over and over again. He will keep calling until you recognize his voice, but it is different for all of us. But God can also speak to us in rest when we are committed to the screenless quiet and stillness.*

*John 4:13 reminds each of us, "And God has given us his Spirit as proof that we live in him and he in us."*

# CHAPTER 15:
## MOVING FORWARD

The first time I tried squats, I thought my legs were going to give out. I couldn't go down very far. Maybe two or three inches, at best. I started out on a 30-inch box, and at first, squatting to this height seemed impossible. I would do 20 to 30 repetitions, go home and cry. Even going to the bathroom was torture. There were so many things my body had never done that every new movement was a bit of a shock.

I told Jamie one morning that I didn't want to be so self-conscious at the gym. I would get embarrassed at almost everything. Although I believed I was concealing it well, I still felt it. She explained to me that embarrassment was a response to the negative reaction we presume people are going to have about us.

"Athena, why do you always think when people look at you, they are looking at you in a negative way?"

Clearly, I had become trapped in my own head. Were people actually paying that much attention to me? How much attention did I pay others in the gym? Not that much. That meant they probably weren't judging me to the degree I assumed.

"Athena, every time you get embarrassed, just refocus your attention. I heard a quote one time and it's the best. It says, 'Relax. The world's not watching that closely. It's too busy contemplating itself in the mirror.'"

Everything she said made perfect sense. I was just going to pretend there wasn't a soul watching. Even if I had to lie to myself, it was just me against me out there.

"God, help me not see anyone when I am there. Make me feel like I am the only one in the room. Help me feel not so self-conscious. I know you are telling me I need to be here, God, and I have listened. But help me with this, please."

I spent hours in my living room some nights learning how to get up off the floor using only my legs and arms. They weren't very strong, so it was tricky at first. But I found what worked. After dozens and dozens of attempts, I could get myself up off the floor. One less thing that was going to make me feel embarrassed. I could do it!

As time progressed, it wasn't unusual for me to cry at night because I was sore. I was tired. I would pray every night I would have the strength to go back and try it one more time. "One more time" eventually turned into weeks.

I had been going to the gym for several weeks and a few of the friends I had met there asked me to take a boot camp class with them. Bootcamp, essentially, was just CrossFit without the barbell. I didn't think I was ready for anything of the sort. I laughed it off during the first invite because I saw what they did in those Bootcamp classes! Even the fit people looked like they were going to keel over after class. But they were persistent.

"Athena, don't worry, we can modify any exercise. You just go at your own pace."

I wasn't even sure what this meant. Go at my pace? By the looks of it, I would still be working on the same set while everyone was finished. I wasn't sure if I liked that idea either. But they were persistent.

I finally gave in and decided to try a Bootcamp session. There was an incredible amount of anxiety leading up to it because I just didn't feel like I could make it through the entire hour.

There was an older woman named Cheryl in the class I had befriended. "Just stick by me, and I will show you what to do," she said. I felt comfortable because I knew someone would be with me, but when I walked in the door that morning I was sweating profusely and so nervous I could have wrung out my shirt before it had even begun.

The music started and I watched Cheryl. Whatever she did, I mimicked. I couldn't do box step-ups, so I just put my leg on the box one at a time. Just lifting my leg up to 24 inches was hard enough. Sit-ups were OK, but I could only do one at a time before I needed to take a breath. I was fine until we moved on to the next movement and found myself trying to get up off the floor. This was a challenge I wasn't prepared for. How do I get up off the floor? I shimmied myself over to the rig so I could use the bars to hoist myself up. I happened to be right next to it. What was going to happen the next time I was out in the middle of the floor? Most people were doing five to fifteen repetitions with every movement, and then we would move on to the next station. I might have done two to five reps during that same period. I felt like I was moving at the speed of a snail, and I couldn't have been more frustrated. I thought I was going to cry in the middle of class, but right when I felt that tears were welling up in my eyes, there was a voice.

"Athena, nice job, keep going!"

Someone is cheering for me? I looked around and there were several people clapping their hands. I forgot about crying and tried my hardest to keep going because now I wanted to do my best for the people who clapped.

"Athena, don't you dare cry. Keep going," said a voice in my head.

When I completed the first class there was a massive sense of accomplishment. I was so proud on my drive home. That feeling was quickly replaced with exhaustion. I slept five hours after I got home and couldn't move my body normally again for nearly three days. I bawled my eyes out on Day 2 because I couldn't walk. Oh, the muscles were so sore. I wanted to quit after that first class because the thought of having to go through that soreness and pain every time I took a class was something I couldn't fathom. You mean to tell me it's going to hurt like this every single time? You have got to be kidding me! This is why I never worked out. I am in pain.

On the third morning after the initial class, my legs were feeling better, and I could move my arms around normally. I sat talking to God with my cup of coffee and said, "God. I am going to keep going, but that really hurt. I suppose it wasn't that bad. Maybe I could try it one more time. God, please help me try it one more time."

That "one more time" turned into several more times. I was now attending a training session or class three times a week. Each class was difficult. I was slow, and I struggled to keep up, which had me crying in the bathroom after class several times. There was nothing more humiliating than huffing and puffing like a horse. I hated it. I took naps almost every single day. There were times I was joyful and other times I was crying my eyes out because of the soreness. Every time I wanted to quit I would look up and pray, "God, just keep me going one more day."

★   ★   ★

In the beginning, I loved working with Kevin. I thought he was a good fit for me, but it didn't last long.

One day I got an invitation to hang out with the 5:30 a.m. class. It sounds silly, and I laugh about it fondly, but these girls were a group all of their own. They were all very fit, so beautiful, I looked up to every one of them — mainly because of their athleticism. I used to watch them in awe; they could do pull-ups and muscle-ups. I knew I could never be like them, but man, the fact they wanted me to hang out with them — that was awesome! Though the 5:30 a.m. class was open to anyone, I almost looked at the morning crew as a secret club. And now I had an invite!

"Athena, come do a class with us!"

I wasn't sure I could handle a CrossFit class, but what was the harm in going? If I could modify a CrossFit class the same way I learned to modify a Bootcamp class, there was no reason to be afraid. I knew if for some reason it got to be too much, I could always sit down and take a break.

I was so excited that I sent a text to Kevin and told him that the girls wanted me to come to a 5:30 a.m. class. I was excited to see what CrossFit was all about.

His response: "Athena, you aren't ready for CrossFit, so I would prefer you not go."

I was a bit taken aback.

Was he serious? I didn't understand what the big deal was. He seemed angry with me and made it clear if I were to continue training with him, I was not to partake in the CrossFit class.

What I wanted was someone to ask me how I felt about it. What did I want to do? I wanted to go to class. I wanted to see what CrossFit was all about. There was a prompt to do CrossFit. Again, I can't describe the prompt other than to say it was the ever-present voice. There was a push to go, and the voice wouldn't shut up about it.

"You can do it, Athena. Don't let anyone get in your way. This will work for you. Trust me. Believe me."

There was a reason I needed to go. I was going to trust my gut and go anyway. Something was telling me there was nothing to fear, so I decided on a compromise. I didn't want to upset Kevin, so I opted to just watch the class. I wouldn't do any physical activity my trainer didn't approve of, but I could still go and see what it was about. It seemed like a win-win.

The next morning, I was sitting on one of the bar stools watching the CrossFit class. I was only watching. Everyone had been right: it's Bootcamp with a barbell. Maybe a little more weight here and there. A few new movements, but nothing seemed crazy. I cheered on the girls and had a good time despite the fact I didn't participate. Kevin was there, participating in class and I got a stern look from him. I knew he was pissed, but I was not participating in the class, so I thought I would be fine.

I was not fine. He came up to me immediately after class was over, pulled me to the side and said we needed to chat.

"Athena, I told you not to come to the class."

"I was only watching; I didn't do the class."

"Athena, I am very smart and I have trained a lot of people. I have a degree. You are nowhere close to being ready for these types of classes."

I just stood there staring at him while he rattled off all his credentials. I had clearly upset him. I wasn't questioning his training, I simply wanted to watch the class and to take part in this invite I had received. For the time being, CrossFit was out of the question. He told me I wasn't ready. I had to believe him. He was my trainer, and at the time, I felt I needed him. I would have to obey and trust he had my best interests at heart.

I desperately wanted the freedom to be able to go in any direction I chose but I didn't want to upset Kevin or lose his trust. I was at a gym meeting lots of new people, and for the first time in a very long time, I had friends. The last thing I wanted to do was cause drama of any kind. I didn't want anyone upset at me, so I kept training with him.

While all of this is going on, I developed a close friendship with Mike, mostly because I saw him nearly every day. The initial disinterest I had became a friendship that turned into a deep appreciation. Whether he knew it or not, he played a role in me getting started. I trusted God. In my mind, I had put all the pieces together. My dreams showed me a gym, it showed me the blond hair girl, it showed me Mike. To me, there was no other reason for him in my life unless he was going to play some kind of significant role in my future. God never told me what kind of role he was going to play, so my mind just took over and created the plan. This was the guy, I guess. Every minute I spent talking with him had me more and more curious about who he was. After a while, I suppose I found him endearing. I knew I liked him, but I never said anything because I feared derailing progress. I was going to continue on my path to health and just see how the whole thing evolved on its own.

One morning I was at the gym before a class having some small talk with Mike. We had both arrived there early because we had come directly from our networking meeting. All a sudden there was an explosion in my head:

"YOU NEED TO TELL HIM YOU LIKE HIM AND YOU NEED TO

TELL HIM TODAY."

This was the most ridiculous thing I had ever heard. One, I wasn't ready to do that. Two, I was fearful. I knew there was a good chance it might not go well. On the other hand, if he is part of my plan somehow, then what's the difference?

The prompt in my head was my own voice but many times it came out of nowhere. I was starting to hear these prompts a lot, and my trust for these prompts was very strong. Because of everything I had seen, I had no reason to doubt it. It was absolutely not what I wanted to do, but I vowed I would do what the voice directed me to do.

I asked him out for coffee. I was shaking, trying to hold back tears as I drove over there to meet him. I had never done anything scarier in my life. One way or the other I was going to get an answer.

He was very surprised, almost shocked. He was kind and very humbled. However, he did not feel the same way. I had never gone out on a limb like that before, and I almost immediately regretted it. Why did I just do that?! He had become such a good friend I was scared that perhaps we wouldn't be friends anymore because I just made it weird.

I was heartbroken. How could I have been wrong? Why would God have shown me this person if he weren't part of my plan? Initially, I was feeling lost and confused. What other possible reason could there have been?

However, something profound did happen. There was this whole other side of me that was incredibly proud of myself. In the past, I would have derailed myself. I would have found the nearest Taco Bell and ate to soothe myself. That didn't happen. I had to talk myself through it, but it didn't happen. I wasn't at this gym because he was there. I cared about my progress, and I was proud of where I was.

JOURNAL ENTRY: JUNE 23, 2017

*I have been given gifts these last six months, and the greatest gift I have discovered is the desire to live my life authentically. I can't possibly be living an authentic life if I am scared or fearful. Power truly comes when despite the outcome of any given situation we can stare our fears in the face. We might stand there shaking and crying, but damn, it can be done. We get so wrapped up in what other people think is best for us, and we get so worried about disappointing people or trying to be the "nice person," that we forget to live for ourselves. I am a Phoenix, rising from the ash. I know this because I just managed to do the bravest thing of my life, and 24 hours later and I am just as solid on my journey as I was yesterday. That's growth, and I couldn't be more proud. Every time I work through a fear I get stronger every day. I wouldn't trade this for anything.*

Three days later, I was sitting in a tattoo chair getting "I AM ENOUGH" tattooed on my forearm with "Matthew 7:7" just below it.

## JOURNAL ENTRY: JUNE 27, 2017

*What defines good enough? It was a profound question I even had to ask myself (again) last week before one random moment I decided to be "Braveheart."*

*For me, my weight determined my value... and for years I let it. Being able to free myself (or working on it) from decades of old, negative self-talk is a journey of recovery that has taken some serious work. I am five years into that part of my journey, and those feelings still surface occasionally.*

*In therapy, I had to work on figuring out where this feeling of "unworthiness" came from. Initially, I tried to deny it, and rationalize and believe that it was all just in my head. Sometimes a bunch of positive affirmations isn't enough. Furthermore, writing a "screw you letter" to the person who first told you that "you weren't good enough" doesn't work either. It just means that the abused now becomes the abuser. No peace comes out of it, trust me. There will never be evidence of "enoughness." Being enough isn't something you need to accrue evidence of, nor do I believe you will ever see proof.*

*Why do we not feel good enough? The comparison is ugly because we are probably comparing ourselves against inaccurate information. Appearances can be deceiving.*

*My new tattoo is about peace. I knew that I would need a reminder so that every time those old, horrid feelings creep back in, I would have it there every day to remind myself that I am indeed "enough." If I have to work on it every day, that's ok.*

*The cross and Matthew 7:7: I have discovered a new life; one that I am tremendously in love with. If you are in doubt right now and need a starting place — "Ask, and it will be given to you; seek, and you will find; knock, and the door will be opened to you."*

Admittedly it took me a while to recognize it. There was one correct interpretation with an infinite number of applications. This guy's role was the door. He was just supposed to open the door. Well it worked because I walked right in.

Some things weren't crystal clear right away, but all the pieces were coming together.

Getting a handle on my weight meant I was going to have to face my fears.

Fears were the root of my weight problem.

I feared change.

I feared physical pain.

I feared working out.

I feared rejection.

I feared upsetting people.

I feared not being good enough.

I feared losing weight. It was all I had ever known. It was my security blanket.

I didn't know it at the time, but God was going to have me face every single fear I ever had.

# LESSON 15

*By Athena Perez with Justin Ghert*

*Be brave enough to be bad at something new.*

*For us, starting CrossFit was like desiring to be a painter but lacking the tools, skills and knowledge. We had to embrace the blank canvas. No expectations, no wondering how many attempts it might take, how hard it would be. Just a naked canvas and full surrender.*

*It was terrifying and uncomfortable. We felt uncertain and inadequate. Had we not determined our "why," we may not have gone back.*

*Our desire for change had to be bigger than the fear and embarrassment. We had to remind ourselves — almost daily — that every day would bring us closer to where we wanted to be.*

*William McRaven gave a speech to the University of Texas graduates in 2014. "Don't back down from the sharks," he said. He talked about enduring a grueling swim through shark-infested waters. It's a good analogy. .*

*Changing your life hurts like hell. Every single day you must battle the sharks swimming in your head, trying to scare you into quitting. There will be days when you feel like you are going to die, but you are going to smack off the sharks and go another day. And then the day after that, and so on. After a while, the sharks don't scare you. You become a shark. And ain't nothing going to get in your way after that.*

# CHAPTER 16:
## *DISCOVERY*

By the end of my third month I was officially cane free.

My legs were still a bit wobbly, and I did use a single cane from time to time, but the improvements to my legs were astounding. I decided I was going to do CrossFit. I was already essentially doing CrossFit, but I wanted to be on that barbell. Damn it, I was going to listen to the voice no matter how crazy it seemed. Every new experience was teaching me to be a little bolder and a little less fearful.

CrossFit seemed impossible. I had a trainer who said I wasn't ready. I had doctors telling me it wasn't possible. The odds were not in my favor, but I knew there was something incredible waiting for me. I knew this because I saw it in my dream. The pull to CrossFit was undeniable.

I was enough, which meant I could do anything I wanted to do. But there was still another hurdle I needed to jump.

I had been playing around with a barbell for several weeks. Most of the time, it was when Kevin wasn't there. I knew he wasn't going to like it. But lifting a barbell seemed to come very naturally. I can't explain it other than I felt like it was something I was supposed to do. I gravitated to it, and I was an excited little kid every time I got around one. One day in the middle of class, we were doing a strength segment that included a barbell. The activity was cleans, which I had very comfortable with. Kevin walked over to me, yanked the barbell out of my hand, and put it back on the wall. He walked a PVC pipe back over to me and said, "I will tell you when you are ready for that."

I guess you could say that was the last straw. I wasn't going to allow someone else to dictate what my future was going to look like. Whether Kevin did it with the best of intentions or not, it had nothing to do with him as a person. It had everything to do with my life.

It was my anger, guilt, shame, embarrassment, resentment and fear — everything I had to work through in order to believe that I could have everything I ever wanted. I was not the girl I used to be. By this time, I had spent six years in therapy. It took six years of difficult work to be able to look myself in the mirror, tell myself I was worth it, that I deserved everything I ever wanted, and actually believe it. I believed that no matter how crazy my idea sounded I could accomplish anything I wanted. At this point, I didn't allow myself to believe something couldn't be done. I would be damned if I let anyone else say that to me. Ever again. Kevin insinuating that I wasn't ready for the barbell I believed was a lie designed to test my newfound resolve in myself.

I took my first CrossFit class in June 2017. It was hard. But it was possible. I wasn't very fast, and I couldn't do much. But I wanted to see what I was capable of. I knew I could do it.

One of my earliest connections in CrossFit was to the "three, two, one, go" countdown used at the start of most classes. My mindfulness exercises often ran through sequences that included purposeful breathing and number counting. I would sit in my favorite chair, breathe slowly, close my eyes, and count to three on the inhale and then back down to zero on the exhale. I did this over and over again, trying to learn how to control my thoughts. The first time I heard that "three, two, one, go," there was a kind of spark of electricity in my brain. I could almost feel the instant energy connection to what I had learned in therapy. And now I was going to get to apply that to my workouts.

Now, I just needed a new coach.

Justin was a CrossFit coach at our gym. He wrote all the programming and taught a majority of the classes. I had watched him for quite a while. I knew when I was ready he would be the person I would talk to. I was nervous about approaching him to be my coach, but I knew he would understand what I wanted. I didn't know where CrossFit could take me, but why couldn't one of those athletes that I watched in the Open or the ones I admired so deeply during the morning classes be me? Why not? What did I have to lose?

Justin was not only a CrossFit coach, but he was also a CrossFit Games athlete. I knew he had never worked with someone who was morbidly obese, and I also knew he never had a weight problem, so understanding some of my challenges wouldn't be possible. However, he had gone to the CrossFit Games. He was part of the one percent of all CrossFit athletes. He didn't understand being morbidly obese, but he did understand what it was like to achieve a massive goal. He had done it. I knew he was the right one.

Once again, as I had always done, I prayed about it. I knew I could do the movements. I felt like it was what I was meant for. There was something so powerful in me that didn't used to be there that said I was not going to let fear stop me ever again. Two days later, I asked him to be my coach, and he agreed.

## JOURNAL ENTRY: JULY 1, 2017

*Day 183. 126 Pounds Lost.*

*Trying to think about six months down the road was far too overwhelming for me. I still don't think that far ahead; I literally take this thing one day at a time. That's what gramps told me to do and so far it's working. This is also how I have found a sense of peace. Ninety-nine percent of the things we think and stress about never happen. Only focusing on today gives me greater control of what I do and the decisions that I make. Time and patience are something that I have embraced (kicking and screaming, yes). I have never been a patient person, nor did I ever practice that virtue on a regular basis. Our environment makes us think that we don't have the time for it. I didn't, and God is teaching me otherwise.*

*January was my Declaration of Independence, and so far I have kept that promise to myself without wavering. This weekend historically has always been a big deal in my family. I have always flown the colors red, white and blue proudly outside my home, and they are playing a role in my life even now. If you didn't know this, white signifies purity and innocence. Red stands for hardiness and valor and blue is for perseverance. I wouldn't exactly say that I am pure and innocent {{laugh}}. However, my intentions from the beginning have been pure, and my desire to rediscover the child inside that seemingly had disappeared have been earnest. Hardiness means that you are able to endure difficult conditions. Any goal requires toughness and stamina, but I never realized until now how difficult it was going to be. I don't know where this monster in my heart came from to tackle this mountain but it's there. I am putting over 900 miles a week in commuting and gym travel, and the gym time itself has become almost like a part-time job on top of every other responsibility. There are times when I am so tired I want to cry, but dammit, I persevere. These are my colors right now. If you want something bad enough, you must fight for it. You will have sacrifices; you will have to give things up. You will miss time with family and friends. You will feel alone. And some days…you will feel like quitting. I can't even begin to imagine what my life would look like had those important men, who fought for our country's independence, had given up. At the same time – I can't imagine what my life would look like if I didn't continue to fight for it.*

As soon as I switched to a new coach, I felt a weight had been lifted.

Sometimes people can still be good people, but they can be the wrong people for us. I felt like I was getting stronger at recognizing this. Does it mean that Kevin was a bad person? No, of course not. He was just the wrong person for me.

In a therapy session shortly after switching coaches, I still felt discontent. I was considering selling my house to move closer to the gym so I could cut down on the 60-mile round-trip commute. My home felt weird to me. For the longest time, it felt like a prison. I was spending less time at home because there was something making me feel uncomfortable. I couldn't put my finger on it, but it became a new topic to talk to God about. What was it about my surroundings that was making me feel uncomfortable? Why did I feel like I was suffocating in my own home?

I prayed about it for several days and the answer appeared in the strangest way. I was doing some organizing and stumbled across a mountain of holiday decorations I had collected over the years. How many holiday decorations does one person need? I had decorations for every single holiday my family celebrated including Easter and Valentine's Day. Decorating for the holidays made me feel good. I hadn't stopped collecting holiday decorations. I had amassed them in every corner of my home.

I felt like I had made a huge discovery about myself.

In The Warrior and The Monk, the young warrior spent a great deal of his life focused on dragons and acquiring treasures of the world: "Yet it seemed to the young warrior the more he focused on dragons, the more dragons appeared within the conditions of his life. And the more the young warrior focused on acquiring treasure, the more treasure he still wanted to have."

This is exactly my experience. I thought that everything I had acquired was to prove I was valuable somehow. My degrees and all my stuff became proof of my accomplishments and became tied to who I was. The voices said I needed to get rid of things, but I didn't like that idea at first. It was scary. All of the things I had kept and collected were a representation of my past life. If I wanted to experience a new life, then I must be willing to let go of the old. That old life was weighing me down.

## JOURNAL ENTRY: JULY 29, 2017

*All the reasons I loved my home when I bought it are starting to weigh me down mostly because the purpose it served then don't serve me today. It was my protection from a very cruel world the heavier I got, but as time went on, it also became my prison. I accumulated "stuff" because this was my sanctuary. That same stuff that made me feel safe has now become clutter.*

*If I dug around, I would find defunct bank statements and cards filled with messages written nearly a decade ago. And then there are the personal items: the crusty bouquet of dried roses I have kept for more than 15 years (a relic from Nick), the giant stack of criminal justice policy books now gathering dust in the corner, the endless piles of birthday cards and letters. I collected and held onto things far too long, and, instead of lifting me up, they have become talismans of shame and guilt. How many things do I need to hold onto before they start controlling my life? They already do. All of my possessions were tied to my self-worth. I have had trouble getting rid of anything that serves as a tangible reminder of my accomplishments. Somehow in my head, all my "stuff" represented how successful my life was. I don't feel the same way anymore, and I didn't realize my clutter is causing actual stress, which is why I want to spend more and more time away from it. Getting rid of things can be scary.*

*My accomplishments aren't going to be tied to "things." I am finding myself this year and realizing I am good enough as is. I will continue this journey in the next few weeks, purging anything I don't need or doesn't serve me. I really have to challenge myself here. It's part of the journey. And…I need to do it #fearlessly.*

*Spiritually, I need to clear the way for things to find me. I am going to trust God on this one because it's what I am being told to do. I don't know why he has given me this assignment, but I will continue to trust him on this journey.*

*In John 15:1-5, Jesus compares Himself to a vine and God to the gardener: "God cuts off every branch that bears no fruit, while every branch that does bear fruit He prunes so that it will be even more fruitful."*

I listened to the prompts and followed the instructions: "Be brave enough to let go." A few weeks later I discovered something else.

## JOURNAL ENTRY: AUGUST 8, 2017

*For whatever reason, I knew when I woke up this morning that today would be the day. I am listening to God. The purging in my home continues, and I knew that I needed to attack the boxes in the bottom of the stairwell. I had tried to do it before, but as soon as I would open the door, I would feel tears, so the door would be quickly shut. Some of the clutter in my home is not so much what you can see. It's the piles and piles of boxes that are stacked in every closet and storage area. However, these boxes were different…I let out a big sigh, and I was already crying before I opened them, but it was time.*

*I have talked about my 11-year relationship many times; these boxes were filled with wedding things, a wedding that I chose to walk away from three months before it was to happen. In December of 2009 when I decided to walk, everything that had been accumulating for the wedding was put into storage bins and taped up around the edges. They made the trip with me from Texas and subsequently were put in the basement when I moved in. There is a part of me that wonders if this was the reason I didn't like spending any time down there. Deep down I knew there was one of the biggest disappointments of my life staring at me every time I had to change my AC filter. Dealing with this loss was the catalyst of my weight gain then. I had already put on about 50 pounds by the time I arrived, but another 120 piled on. Well, at least 120 anyway. I don't think I will ever know the true number.*

*As I cut the duct tape from the first box, my heart was in knots. "Athena, you can do this," I whispered to myself.*

*When the lid was removed, I sat there staring blankly at the neatly packed box full of all of the little things that I had poured my heart into. Extra Invitations, card labels, table cards, favors, menu cards…all of the accessories for the ceremony and reception. Even the cake toppers that were meticulously selected because both people were on the phone, a representation of our life at that time. Those little cake toppers didn't seem so funny anymore.*

*I only ended up keeping one item from these boxes: a pair of white silk flats with ballerina laces. For whatever reason I still loved them.*

*I kept all of these things because I hoped that someday I would get married. Perhaps there was a part of me that thought if I got rid of everything that wouldn't happen, so rather than get rid of this stuff back in '09, I thought it would be better if I just clung to them. It wasn't healthy. When that time comes again, then all the planning needs to be fresh with the person that will be forever. New colors, new memories. I can't start something new if I am clinging to something old.*

*Getting past yesterday demands both thinking and doing. It's not just things we do but things we think as well that hold us unknowingly in a very painful place. The idea of letting go forces us to go up against our three craziest, most powerful emotional drivers: love, fear and rage.*

*God told me it wasn't up to me. Surrendering and fully trusting in HIM is hard. I will trust.*

*God, I don't like this. But I am going to trust you. You haven't let me down yet.*

A few days later, I made another big discovery while my parents were at my house.

At this point, my folks were living in Minnesota and visiting every weekend, so my dad, the superhero contractor, could help me with maintenance projects around the house. While he did that, mom and I would go through every single room, purging my needless collections. There was so much stuff. It was a huge job that required several people. We cleaned out everything from closets to drawers, clothing, knick-knacks, even furniture. That particular weekend, it was time to lay the new hardwood floors in my bedroom.

Right before that, I was sitting in the middle of the room, staring up at my walls. I realized 90 percent of the room's décor involved the "Titanic." It's not that I didn't know this. I mean, I had collected all of it myself. But I didn't realize there was a huge tie to my past in this room. There was everything from menu cards to pictures of the ship before it left port, an old ticket and newspaper clippings. Most people called this little collection rather morbid. I will admit it was, but there was a deeper meaning behind it all. "Titanic" was the movie Nick and I saw on our first date. So, in a silly way, it became part of our story. No surprise that it became the theme of our bedroom. Over the years, even long after our separation, I was still collecting "Titanic" stuff. I didn't realize there was still so much of "us" in my home.

As I went through the room, I started finding pictures and upside-down frames under the bed and in every hidden space in the room. I suppose there was a part of me that thought if he were out of sight, he would be completely out of mind. But this wasn't true. My past life had been staring at me, and I didn't know it. Our life was everywhere — not just under the bed, but all over the room and it had to go. It was time to pull the sinking ship off the walls. There was so much irony in this it's almost funny. Afterward, I hand-selected a few new pictures and shelves, and I can't tell you how nice it was. That ship wasn't exactly inspiring me.

After my bedroom was done, I moved to the office. There, I had a letter tote. It was a big deal to me because it contained every single card and letter I had ever received since 1998. I only got about a half-inch in when I stumbled across a nice written card saying thank you for something, and it was signed by someone I didn't even remember. I then came across an old "I love you" card. That's when I refused to go any further. How much energy was this tote carrying? There was only one thing to do. Burn it.

I believe in releasing energy. And that tote burned to ashes.

It took several minutes while I took deep breaths and walked down the stairs and out to the burn pit. Somewhere in this box were my cards from my grandparents, written in their hand. How could I possibly throw them away?! It was gut-wrenching. But into the fire they went. I thought I would start crying. But I stood there, watched the fire and played, "We Didn't Start the Fire," by Billy Joel in my head. I knew I didn't need paper cards to remind me how much they loved me and I them. The memories don't die when you let things go.

Memories and stuff are not the same. It was a huge lesson. Huge.

After the letter tote burned, I was having my morning coffee. I looked up and said, "OK, God, what's next? What do I need to heal next?"

He was giving me confirmation after confirmation. I had NO reason to doubt any of it.

# LESSON 16

*It is so dang powerful to say, "This is what I want," and firmly stand by it. To make a steadfast commitment to yourself, to stand by that promise. It is so empowering.*

*Success at anything isn't necessarily because we are exceptionally smart or lucky. Rather the foundation is set when you firmly outline a set of commitments and see them through.*

*It doesn't mean the path is linear. You're probably not going to get a set of fancy directions or an elusive treasure map that hints at where you should go. That path is going to be riddled with twists and forks. And most likely, it might punch you in the mouth a few times.*

*Figure out what you want, declare it, stand firm and decide to keep moving forward no matter what.*

# CHAPTER 17:
## APPLY WHAT YOU'VE LEARNED

By August 2017, I had lost 150 pounds.

I was learning tons of abbreviations, including PR (personal record), AMRAP (as many rounds as possible) and EMOM (every minute on the minute). I kind of felt like I had been invited to a secret club and I loved it.

My gym community was a culture all its own and also spoke its own language.

"Athena, stop calling it a 'gym.' It's a 'box."

"A box? Why? Is that because it's, like, a rectangle or square?"

That was met with laughter.

## JOURNAL ENTRY: AUGUST 18, 2017

*My body likes the barbell, and any exercise having to do with that bar, so I tend to gravitate to that. I find joy in pushing my body to find out what it's capable of. And yes, I have heard it all, "Athena, you might hurt yourself." I suppose there is a possibility in anything, but you know what was hurting me? The woman I used to be. That hurt me. Joy is finding that I always seem to have a little more to give...*

When I first heard my grandpa talking to me in my dreams, he said, "Athena, take it one day at a time." A common phrase in the CrossFit methodology is, "Take it one rep at a time." I knew I was where I needed to be. Finding that I always had a little more to give was life-changing because the meaning behind it wasn't just impacting what I was learning in the box, it was something I could take into my everyday life. CrossFit wasn't just transforming me physically; it was transforming how I looked at life. It's the idea that I could do anything I wanted — one rep at a time.

If I wanted to learn how to lift heavy, it was one rep at a time. If I wanted to hit a big sequence of squats, it was one rep at a time. When I thought a workout was too difficult, and I thought about giving up, it was one rep at a time.

As I took this outside the box, it sounded like this: get through my task lists, clean my house, write a book — one rep at a time. In my outside life, it really became more of an expression of potential. All I had to do was focus on one rep at a time. It became one of the most important things I learned.

"Embrace the darkness" was also a phrase I heard frequently in class. What is the darkness? A dark place is somewhere we have all been. I had been there many times in life, but one experience took place over one Christmas, lying in the middle of the living-room floor, thinking my legs had finally given out. I was screaming at God to just "let it all be over." I was done. At that moment, I questioned everything in my life. I even wondered whether my life was worth living. There was nobody else around; it was just me against me. Now, of course, I credit God for helping me out of that dark place; we've all been there. I was able to live through it and discovered there was a life worth living the following day. But being in that dark place made me stronger. Some of us have been in that dark place many times. Each time we visit, we come out just a little stronger on the other side.

In your workouts, that dark place is when it hurts, it burns, and you think you cannot give any more. Maybe there is a little fear and a little doubt. There is no ounce of energy left, and there is a good chance you might have tears running down your face. But in that dark place, you hear "one more rep." And one grueling rep after the next, you climb out of the dark and the workout is complete. Believe it or not, there were more days like this than not when I started moving. But it was teaching me that no matter how hard or difficult it was, I would always finish. And it made me stronger every single time. Not just physically, but mentally.

The minute I walked out of the box I was ready for life. I would get through the most grueling workout. That tough day at work? No problem. It became something I craved because it always set me up for a successful day. No matter what came up during my day, it was typically nothing close to what I went through that morning. Everything just became a little more tolerable.

Right around the time when I learned what "embrace the darkness" meant, I was having a very tough time during one of my workouts. Perhaps I was a little burnt out. I embraced the suck of the grind, as I called it, but it was exhausting — the daily time investment, the 60-plus-mile round-trip commute, the soreness. I fell asleep right in the middle of the gym on the green carpet. I thought, "God, I don't know how long I can do this. Help me — because I want to quit."

I awoke to one of the coaches turning on the music. The first song I heard was "Hard Love" by a band called NeedtoBreathe.

The lyrics just got me. I felt like the song was speaking to me at that very moment because it recognized the darkness I felt and the help I needed from God. As I continued to listen to the song, I felt like it was the voice not only answering my prayer but delivering in a way that I needed to hear it.

The song basically said If I wanted a big change, I needed to burn that old person away. The burn was through my workouts, through that place of darkness I had to learn to embrace. It was almost as if it was confirmation I was doing the right thing, using the right tools. The chorus was essentially saying, "Hey, if it doesn't kill you, it's going to make you stronger. No matter how down you feel, you have to keep getting back up and live to do it another day, and you have to be willing to do it over and over again. Courage is like a muscle and if you are going to make it strong as hell you have to exercise it every day; you need it for the journey."

This song became my anthem. Every single day I would wake up and play this song on my drive. It never got old because I felt like the message was for me. It didn't matter how many times I heard it because it was reminding me that it was one day at a time, one rep at a time. Keep going.

Back in the box, every new training session with Justin was exciting. We figured it out together. I was new to every movement, and he was new to coaching someone like me. Neither of us knew the exact "best" ways to modify movements, but we figured it out one movement at a time. If something wasn't working, we would drop weight or decrease the distance to an object. If something was working well, we would add weight and increase the distance to an object. Sometimes improvements meant adding more time, adding more weight, adding more repetitions. Every session seemed to indicate noticeable improvements from one week to the next, and many times the joy was measured only in laughter and hugs and high fives. The more improvements I made, the more we worked. When a skill was mastered, we would move on to the next or turn up the intensity.

One day I was working alone on the rower and Justin had arrived to teach a class. He walked over and asked what I was doing.

"Well, I gotta finish the rower first. I have about 2,000 meters to go. And then after that, I gotta…" I started.

Justin put his hands up to his chin, nodding as I rattled off what I had to do. Then, he replied.

"Athena, you don't have to do it. You get to do it."

Saying something as simple as "I have to" changed the way I looked at the work. It stung like a bee because it was so profound at that moment. A simple shift to "I get to" made it so empowering.

Every time I picked up a piece of equipment, got on a bike or rower, or went to grab the barbell, I would whisper that phrase. "I don't have to, I get to."

★　　★　　★

Do I think a path forward was provided by divine intervention because He knew it would be effective? I do.

CrossFit was a form of therapy all its own. The lessons I was learning almost daily were applicable in and outside the box, just like sitting in my favorite chair in my therapist's office. The minute I left Jaime's office, there was always something to think about or something to apply. It had immediate, measurable results. The CrossFit methodology is very much the same way, which is the reason I believed it connected with me.

When I say immediate, measurable results, I don't necessarily mean that my muscles suddenly stacked, and I could snatch 300 lbs. It was more spiritual for me because fear was my biggest weakness. Tackling that fear meant I needed to dedicate time to working on myself and tackling those weaknesses head-on. But more significantly, I needed to be OK with where I was on any given day. After all, showing up was half the battle. Those workouts were opportunities to attack my most significant physical weaknesses. Instead of avoiding them, I could survive the nightmare and be grateful for the fact I could improve the following day again. There was always something I could improve on. The list was never-ending.

I didn't have to compete with anyone. I had my path when it came to my goals and I got to honor those. I didn't have to keep up with others because I wanted their success. I got to go after my own. I could genuinely run my own race.

I had experienced a lot of challenges in my life, and my previous life always seemed so hard. Every day was a struggle. But, showing up every day and committing to doing the work was teaching me that not all hard things are bad. Let's face it: CrossFit workouts are hard. But they aren't bad. I might have cried my way through many of them, but the accomplishment I felt when the buzzer sounded was something I had never felt. I was so proud. That pride created confidence and a bucket of self-worth that did not previously exist.

# LESSON 17

*By Athena Perez with Dave Eubanks*

*Change the daily dialogue.*

*Every action we take begins as a thought.*

*It is therefore incumbent on us to at the very least understand these thoughts, and at best, control them — to harness them to work for us rather than against us.*

*Changing the daily dialogue doesn't happen overnight.*

*It is a process rife with pitfalls, setbacks and wrong turns. However, the fact that the journey is difficult makes it worthwhile. Growth requires adversity.*

*You'll find this adversity everywhere you look when striving for improvement. You'll find it when your favorite show is on late at night, but you KNOW you need a good night's sleep to feel your best tomorrow. You'll feel it when your favorite dessert stares at you as you walk past it at the grocery store.*

*There are many ways to change your internal dialogue.*

*Maybe you tell yourself, "I can do this."*

*Maybe you say, "I deserve this."*

*Maybe someone tells you, "You don't have to do this; you get to do this."*

*Maybe it just starts with someone showing you that they believe in you.*

*Be aware of your thoughts. Understand where they come from, and use that knowledge to cultivate the thoughts you want and cull the ones you don't.*

# CHAPTER 18:

## *VALUE THE PROCESS*

About a month later, I saw an ad on Facebook for an event called Rugged Maniac, an annual obstacle course race.

"Participants run a five-kilometer course with obstacles ranging from muddy water slides, crawling through tunnels, jumping over logs set on fire, and scaling a large curved wall," according to Rugged Maniac.

In my mind, I wasn't ready for anything like this, but I kept seeing the ad. It was almost as if it kept jumping out at me. A race? I wasn't going to beat anyone in the race. I was scared I wouldn't be able to finish. I still had trouble even walking a 5K, let alone tackling obstacles through uneven terrain and mud. It was clear there was fear, but fear of what?

As usual, I took it to Jamie for further dissection.

"Why do I fear something like this? Is it because I won't finish?"

"You fear it because it's a perceived danger. After all, Athena, you have been told your whole life you can't do things like this. But there's such great value in this."

"What do you mean there's value? What kind?"

"Fear has power because you allow it. Every time you are bold enough to face whatever it is you fear, you become stronger. When you acknowledge the fear, but do the opposite, you become more courageous."

I wanted to be courageous. At this point, I wanted to hunt down every fear I had and slice its throat. I would never let fear run my life again. I prayed about it.

The voice said, "Face your fears."

I was scared, but I did it anyway. I trusted God so much, I knew I would be taken care of. It didn't mean it was going to be easy for me, but it meant that I wasn't by myself.

## JOURNAL ENTRY: SEPTEMBER 17, 2017

*Every step of the last mile hurt, and it was painful. I think that there is a part in all of us that dislikes being so vulnerable. The simple idea of letting other people see me shake, struggle, and cry...when I am at my worst is tough. Uhhg. Giving up wasn't an option, but I did wonder if my legs were just going to stop moving. I was feeling a bit of anxiety and perhaps embarrassed that I was last. At one point I got the "30-minute warning;" they were going to close the course. "I am sucking aren't I," was all I thought that last half-mile. I said a prayer in my head that sounded a bit like, "Fine, they can see me struggle but please God don't let them see me fall." I didn't fall…I am grateful for that.*

*I had witnessed people being taken down off that mountain yesterday, and I wasn't one of them. Granted I didn't try every single obstacle, but I finished. The support was immense, and I feel so much gratitude today it's unbelievable. I didn't do as well as I wanted, and it took much longer than I thought it would, but I finished. Face the fear and finish; that's the only goal I had.*

*All I could think about today was how much better I know I can do next year. I am not afraid of these events anymore, so that fear is gone.*

Doing regular burpees was a struggle because there was fear. Part of the fear was not being able to get up; part of the fear was not understanding how to connect all the moving pieces.

One day during training, I told Justin I wanted to learn how to do burpees, but I was afraid that I couldn't.

"Athena, you can totally do these. Let's break them down. You can get down on the ground, right?"

"Yes."

"OK, that's one movement. You can do a push-up right?"

"Yes."

"OK, that's movement No. 2. You can get off the ground doing a push-up right?"

"Yes."

"So, what are you afraid of?"

It seemed silly. I could do all the things he mentioned, but for some reason I was afraid. But as I was learning, the only way to comfort my heart was for my brain and body to show it that I could.

"OK, Athena, get down on the ground. Now, take your hands and push-up off the ground! OK, now you are up. Now kick your feet and pull yourself up."

I had done a burpee! A real one!

Learning I could do more and more inspired me to make the wish lists bigger. If I could learn how to do a burpee, maybe I could learn to lift really heavy! Six weeks later, I was able to hit a 300 pound deadlift.

## JOURNAL ENTRY: DECEMBER 18, 2017

*If you had asked me back in my twenties what the "Seven Wonders of the World" were I would have said the Statue of Zeus at Olympia, or maybe the Great Pyramid of Giza. I have learned this year that the things we overlook as simple or what we take for granted are truly amazing! A gentle reminder — life's greatest treasures cannot be bought. The journey was to experience the Seven true Wonders of life. Only through this would I understand how to move forward.*

*To see. I feel that I was given the gift of being able to see life with a new set of eyes. I was able to see things my body could do that I never thought possible. I was able to see the birth of a new part of my life: health and fitness. Obviously, these are two things I never thought would be part of my permanent being. I was able to see physical change and the accomplishment of goals. I was able to see the start of new passions and new directions for my life.*

*To hear. I feel that my relationship with God is one that improved significantly, and I learned how to listen. I will admit that even today I don't always understand what I hear, but nonetheless, the voice is there. Sometimes it comes through a dream, other times it comes through inspired thought. But there is always that little nudge that keeps me going and points me in the right direction. That voice was there January 1st when I was on my knees asking God for help. The voice said not to be afraid, and the answer would be provided. It didn't fail me.*

*To touch. I could go in a few directions on this one, but I will tell you the best feeling in the world; the hugs, the high fives and those fist bumps of encouragement that I have received this year have been tremendous. Every single one of them helps.*

*To taste. Eating for fuel instead of eating out of boredom or misery has been a game-changer. Eating clean completely changed my palette. My cravings for sugar and poison are no more. My body craves things like carrots, kale, apples, nuts and strawberries. I feel like I can actually taste food now. The difference in my face and skin says a lot about the food I put in my body. The proof is visual everywhere. My relationship with food is improving. It's not perfect. But I am learning.*

*To Feel. It's hard to describe life one year ago, but I can tell you it was a dark place.*

*I feel everything now mostly because I am not fearful of HOW I feel anymore. I am not afraid to express how I feel, and I am not afraid to talk about it.*

*To Laugh. Laughing as well as "feeling" is hard when you feel like shit. This year has provided more laughs in my life than I can remember. I am not talking about simple giggles; I am talking about the bellyaching-laughing-till-I-pee-my-pants kind of laughing.*

*To Love. I have always loved with my heart and not my eyes which I believe is a blessing, but when you go through devastating relationships or breakups, life has a way of hardening your heart. I have loved fiercely this year. Mostly, myself.*

*These seven things really are the wonders of life. This journey has been about finding these things through a certain appreciation for life and a deeper level of awareness. I am blessed. Far more than I could ever express here.*

At the stroke of midnight on December 31, 2017, I had lost 187.5 pounds. You would think I would have been overjoyed — and I was — but there was a part of me that was disappointed. This all-or-nothing side of me that clearly was not completely healed reared its ugly head and during a time when I should have been proud, I was upset. I didn't reach my goal of 200 pounds lost.

I spent weeks agonizing over the fact I fell short. Damn it, I was so close! After two months of rolling my sorrows into spoonfuls of peanut butter and not making any progress, this is what came out in my journal:

## JOURNAL ENTRY: FEBRUARY 1, 2018

*Self-reflection is something I regularly do. Maybe I didn't do a lot of that previously because I was too prideful to admit that the problem was ME. If someone had told me a year ago that this journey wouldn't be about weight loss, I wouldn't have believed them. I thought weight loss was the whole point?*

*For a while there I got caught up in the numbers when in reality this expedition is about growth. The reason I got up to almost 500 pounds had everything to do with pride, jealousy, ego, guilt, shame, blame, poor self-image, lack of confidence, despair, depression, hopelessness…(insert mile-long list here). The weight problem was a consequence of these things. If you want to get to the root of your weight problem (or some other kind of addiction), you need to get to the heart of what caused it in the first place. Most of us don't want to admit that our challenges in life or problems with others are a direct reflection of how we FEEL about ourselves.*

*One of my worst downfalls in life has been pride. I never let anyone help me with my weight problem growing up because I was too embarrassed to say I didn't have it figured out.*

*"Poor self-worth and shame drive pride. We feel so badly about ourselves that we compensate by feeling superior or…we look for others' flaws as a way to conceal our own. Pride prevents us from acknowledging our human vulnerabilities" (Amodeo, J). My weight was a problem my entire adult life because of pride. I know that now.*

Despite being disappointed that I didn't hit my goal, I competed in my first CrossFit Games Open in February 2018. The girl who walked into a box with two canes actually did it.

I was scared of signing up, but I did it. I saw it as a place of darkness. If I can face the fear and get through it, then I know I can get through anything. I had never felt more physically accomplished in my life. It didn't matter that I was in the bottom 50 percent of all sign-ups. It didn't matter that I knew I wouldn't win. It was simply the idea that I could even be included at all — that I could get out there and do my best just like everyone else. To feel included and to feel accepted. To be able to look at myself in the mirror as I was getting ready for workout No. 1 with my Open T-shirt on and say, "Girl, you are enough," and believe it. It was all worth it.

Not hitting my goal taught me about the pride and ego I was still carrying around. Pride and ego were not on my initial "work-on" list, but I discovered I needed to address them as well.

"It has been said that your ego will deceive you by edging God out." -- Greg Amundson

Not hitting the goal taught me something else: Far more powerful than simply hitting some magic target, I had the wrong values. I forgot about the journey, the purpose of my walk that God had me on. God didn't care about the numbers.

# LESSON 18

*By Athena Perez with Mike Koslap*

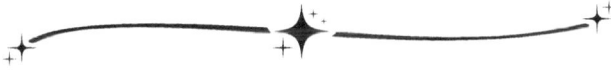

---

*Value the process. Not the goal.*

*By default, we are wired to be goal-pursuing, results-focused people. Why? Because the result is so much easier to evaluate than the processes taken to get there. We judge ourselves based on results, and we care what others think.*

*Only focusing on outcomes can make you miserable because you go through the stages of grief each time you don't hit one. This grief promotes terrible habits and can turn your thinking toxic. But focusing on process rather than outcome is a much better strategy.*

*The process allows you to experiment and have fun! When you're so focused on the goal, you're less willing to try to new things, or even better yet, be open to ideas and maybe even stumble across something that might work better.*

*Focusing on the process also allows us to live in the present and enjoy the tiny victories along the way - the ones you might not have noticed before.*

*Happiness is not a destination.*

# CHAPTER 19:
## SHARE WHAT YOU KNOW

In March 2018, my life as I knew it would change forever.

I got an email from CrossFit Inc. asking if I would be willing to be filmed for a CrossFit Journal story on my weight loss success. Of course, I agreed.

This simple request would put into motion a series of unfathomable experiences. There were still unknowns about my dreams, but I would find them all.

## JOURNAL ENTRY: MARCH 18, 2018

*The guy that was here doing the filming asked some very thoughtful questions. To be honest, I hadn't thought about many of them. Life simply evolved. One of them was the question about these canes I used to leave all over the house so that I could have something to brace my body against the minute I left the comfort of my stable kitchen counters. As I was holding one of these canes, I saw flashbacks of me trying to walk with these things, and I felt the pain in my legs as if it were yesterday. There were days I tried to stumble around wondering when the pain was going to stop. These memories echoed around in my head as I sat there staring at them for the first time since they got put away. I had forgotten. How could I have, it wasn't even that long ago? It brought a level of gratitude I had never experienced before.*

*I feel unbelievably blessed today remembering some of these life experiences that got me right here. I have no idea what the result of this interview will be. What parts will they keep and how will it flow or come together? I have no clue. I will be surprised like everyone else. I won't even get to see a cut before it airs, so I am a bit nervous about that. However, the simple fact I can share my life with others is a blessing and I am grateful. I wonder how many people out there are just like I was: scared of being judged, scared that they won't have the support and more importantly, afraid to just…open the door. If my story can help one person — mission accomplished.*

I was nervous about telling the entire world even the tiniest back story because, initially, I was worried I would have to tell the rest of it. At the time, I didn't want to, and it brought a lot of stress. I had worked through most of it in therapy, but that didn't mean I wanted the world to know.

Secondly, some of those feelings I was still working on — and continue to work on today. Healing is a long road.

Throughout it all, that voice that had remained so vigilant kept saying,

"Face the fear, it will be OK."

After the Journal story and podcast were published, there was a communication frenzy in my inbox. There were so many people reaching out. I would respond to 20, 30 or 40 messages at night and by morning they had all but been replaced by new ones. I was grateful beyond measure, but the stress of trying to respond to every single person broke my heart. I didn't want them to think the time they took to send me such a heartfelt message was simply getting tossed aside. There were just too many.

The messages were inspiring. Some people shared their stories, others were simple congratulations. But in so many of them, I was hearing the same word.

"Athena, you are a hero."

A hero? I felt inadequate, undeserving of such a title. That brought stress of its own because I didn't feel I deserved any of that. I was not alone on my journey.

The stress of trying to write thousands of emails was getting the best of me. Some of the content of the emails were getting difficult for me to deal with. And I sometimes felt I was not qualified to be giving advice. I was honored they came to me, but I didn't know how to direct them. Some of them I simply didn't know how to help.

Sometimes, if too much change happens too quickly, your mind just shuts down. That's exactly what mine did. It was too much, too fast. I had just quit my job, which was an incredibly scary jump for me. I was nervous, I was scared. I noticed I would annoy easily, I was getting short with people, and it wasn't me. It was a signal that something was out of place. I knew I wanted to write; I even knew what the voice was telling me to write about, but I didn't know where to start. I was hoping the few days of downtime in California might help answer some of my questions.

When I went back to California at the end of June to take my CrossFit Level 1 Certificate Course, I got several of the answers I searched for over a year.

During my CrossFit Level 1, I was followed most of the weekend for filming so they could showcase more of the journey. I was outside collecting dirt to send to a few Australian affiliates that had requested it. I am laughing and holding this sandy dirt in my hands. Instantly, I had a flashback.

In the series of dreams, I was holding sand and laughing. Well, it had happened once again — confirmation for me that what I had seen was real. It was real.

The second flashback was on my way home. I was about three-quarters of the way through The Warrior and The Monk. I set the book down and just started thinking about everything that happened over the last year and a half. My whole CrossFit experience was racing through my mind like a freight train and then attending this seminar and running into Greg Amundson. I remember sitting in my seat; I said a prayer.

"God, is there a learning lesson here? What is my takeaway today?"

I went back to reading.

I was driving home from the airport when I happened to see a church billboard that simply read, "1 Peter 2:9." I looked it up when I got home.

"...that you may declare the praises of him who called you out of darkness into his wonderful light."

I sat there pondering this scripture for quite some time.

It was all clear.

This next chapter was to be my testimony. God had called me out of darkness into a life I could not have imagined or accomplished on my own. I knew this to be true. However, I didn't feel qualified to spread this message. I felt God might have chosen the wrong person and that was the reason I was struggling. I didn't want the job. I hadn't reached my weight goal yet. I didn't believe I had entirely healed yet because parts of the old me still surfaced.

"No, God, please not me. I am not ready for this. I can't."

I felt the people who were called to bear testimony of God's greatness were reserved for the special — like the magnificent pastor at my church and pastors at churches all across America. Greg Amundson — he was one of the chosen. These were the chosen.

I cuss like a sailor — something I ask for forgiveness daily. Empathy is still a struggle, I can still get ticked off quickly and it's not uncommon for me to have severe anxiety. How on Earth was this to be my mission? Certainly, there was someone out there 10 times more qualified to talk to people about God than me. I felt unworthy.

At the same time, I couldn't stop thinking about the items on this lofty list I had given God the year before. One by one every single one of them was materializing in some way. Every single thing I saw in those dreams had come to pass. There were even confirmations along the way that kept telling me that everything I heard and saw was real.

While I was struggling with the idea of this book and not really wanting to do it, I received a Facebook message one night. It was from the band Needtobreathe. One of the members had seen my video and responded only with, "Way to go, Athena!" I had a million confirmations up to this point, but I think this is where it solidified it for me. There was God again, reminding me that I was on the right path. Was I afraid of letting people into part of my life I had never talked about? Horrified, actually. But my belief in God and the miracle he did for me is bigger than that fear.

In the end, this journey of mine became less about losing weight as much as it had to do with learning to develop a personal relationship with God. I had figured out who I was, and simply put, I was a child of God. I never had to hit a pie-in-the sky goal to feel peace, to feel happy. It was never the weight that was dragging me down. It was all the feelings I waited to confront. I see the "wait" as the time I spent healing. The healing that was desperately needed so I would have the mental strength needed to start the next chapter. Only when I learned to trust God did I begin to heal because the source of my healing was God. Only when I learned to listen was I able to work through the demons and dragons that created a barrier between who I was and who I wanted to be.

So, here I am. I have lost over 200 pounds and the journey continues, but it was never about the weight. I thought it was at first. But it wasn't. The biggest lesson I learned was that losing weight was not the purpose of the journey. Sure, it was a positive outcome of the things I had learned, but it wasn't the purpose of the road God was having me walk. I truly believe he was more interested in healing my heart first. I didn't know it several years ago, but without the initial healing of my mind and heart, there was no way healing of the body could begin. Healing of the body is an entirely different journey and one I feel has only just begun. I haven't reached my goals yet, but I continue to walk the road of learning to better my relationship with food daily. God hasn't left my side. He has shown me many other lessons though; some just couldn't fit into this book. I suppose I am writing that chapter now.

I also think God wanted to help me find him, and through him I would be able to find myself. My source. Everything I went through — even the things that never made it into this book — gave me courage, hope, strength and built my faith. Some might say all of it was a coincidence. "Athena, they were just silly dreams." I am prepared for that.

In September 2018, I was asked to give a seminar on my journey at a local gym. My friend Dennis snapped a picture of me while I was speaking so I would have something to remind me of this day. I was pulling images off the camera later that evening and posted an image on Instagram. Once it had been published, I sat there staring at it for a few minutes. The scene looked oddly familiar and then I remembered where I had seen it. That was me. The "me" that appeared in the first set of dreams I had in January 2017.

"I didn't recognize myself. I could tell it was me because of my face, but my eyes looked different."

They looked happy.

My eyes do look different. They do look happy. But that doesn't mean I don't still make bad decisions and that guilt, shame, embarrassment, resentment and fear never surface. They do all the time. There is still more to learn. God continues to walk with me every step of the way. That is what makes me happy — knowing that if I continue to seek God first, everything else will be added.

"Young warrior, I believe unconditionally in you and your ability to succeed. Commit to your Sadhana, trust in God, and when you are ready, teach these principles to all those whom you hold dearly in your life." -- The Warrior and the Monk

I am ready.

# LESSON 19

*By Athena Perez with Rory McKernan*

*Being vulnerable isn't easy, but it can change people's lives.*

*When we only share our highlight reels, it sends a message to others that they, too, can only share the good things in their lives. But when we share the messy, no-so-perfect and complicated parts of our stories, we start to find our people — the ones who get and understand us. When we embrace our imperfections, it's a chance for us to not only connect but build trust. We also create a safe space for others to share, and we create awareness that we are not alone. It serves as a reminder that there are others out there — some just like you, some who you look up to and admire — who bleed red just like the rest of us.*

*Sharing the pain and suffering that extends beyond exercise is lighter fluid to the fire of this compassion. Those who have felt loss, devastation, grief and pain find solace in a community that loves them both for who they are and who they have the potential to be.*

*Our's is a community joined by shared physical suffering in the pursuit of optimizing health. It's a recreational pursuit, but the bonds forge fast and run deep, strengthened by our daily practice of facing self-imposed adversities.*

*In both sport and training applications, we become uniquely empathetic as a group — we truly feel one another. We support each other in triumphs, and we share in the failures because our understanding comes from having been there ourselves.*

*"Telling our stories is not an end in itself, but an attempt to release ourselves from them, to evolve and grow beyond them" -- Rachael Freed.*

# EPILOGUE

Brad passed away three months after I started writing this book. He had a heart attack on September 11, 2018. It was a rough day for me. That tiny piece of hope I held onto for some reconciliation with him was gone. I had sent him that horrible letter years ago. I never apologized for that. It was my truth when I sent it, but it was also done to hurt him. I wanted him to feel some of the hurt I had felt my whole life.

It has taken a lot of years to be able to recover positive memories about my father. There are few. I remember his laugh and that he loved polar bears. I remember he used to play guitar and listen to Dan Fogelberg and Christopher Cross. Every time I hear "Ride Like the Wind" by Christopher Cross on the radio, I smile. Brad loved "Star Wars." The original movie was released two weeks before I was born in the late seventies. Brad and my mom saw it several times before I was born and many more times thereafter.

I forgave Brad years ago, but I struggled for several months after his death. Maybe I just wanted to say goodbye. I prayed to God that I would be able to find a peaceful way to let him go once and for all. In December 2019 I got that opportunity.

I had just bought two movie tickets to Star Wars: The Rise of Skywalker. I was intending to go with Dennis, but I had forgotten he would be overseas visiting his sister. I pondered who I would take to the theater and considered calling a close friend, but the night before the movie I was thinking about Brad and broke down. I sat in my chair and talked to him the same way I talk to God every day. I told him I forgave him, that I loved him, and that I was taking him to the movies with me.

The next day I was actually excited. I didn't take a friend with me. That movie ticket was for Brad. I always get cold sitting in that freezing theater, so I packed up my blanket and drove over there with the two tickets in my pocket.

I sat down in my seat, pushed the recliner button till my legs were up and comfy and then spread the blanket across myself and the empty seat beside me. I set a few twizzlers and a handful of popcorn down on the chair and smiled as the movie was beginning. A few times during the movie I would look over and smile. It almost felt like he was with me that day. I believe he was.

RESOURCES

# HOW DO I REPORT SUSPECTED CHILD ABUSE OR NEGLECT?

Contact your local child protective services office or law enforcement agency.

Childhelp National Child Abuse Hotline

Call or text 1-800-4-A-CHILD (1-800-422-4453).

Professional crisis counselors are available 24 hours a day, 7 days a week, in over 170 languages. All calls are confidential. The hotline offers crisis intervention, information and referrals to thousands of emergency, social service and support resources.

# HOW DO I REPORT SUSPECTED DOMESTIC VIOLENCE?

Contact your local law enforcement agency.

National Domestic Violence Hotline

1-800-799-SAFE (7233).

The National Domestic Violence Hotline's highly trained advocates are available 24/7/365 to talk with anyone affected by domestic violence. The Hotline provides lifesaving tools, safety planning, immediate support and hope to empower victims to break free of abuse. Resources and help can be found at thehotline.org or by calling 1-800-799-SAFE (7233).

(The National Domestic Violence Hotline, 2020)

# HOW DO I REPORT A SEXUAL ASSAULT?

Contact your local law enforcement agency.

National Sexual Assault Hotline

1-800-656-HOPE (4673).

Its free. Its confidential. It's available 24/7.

RAINN (Rape, Abuse & Incest National Network) is the nation's largest anti-sexual violence organization. RAINN created and operates the National Sexual Assault Hotline (800.656.HOPE, online.rainn.org y rainn.org/es) in partnership with more than 1,000 local sexual assault service providers across the country and operates the DoD Safe Helpline for the Department of Defense. RAINN also carries out programs to prevent sexual violence, help survivors, and ensure that perpetrators are brought to justice.

# WORKS CITED

Amodeo, John. "Why Pride Is Nothing to Be Proud Of." *Psychology Today*, Sussex Publishers, June 6, 2015, www.psychologytoday.com/intl/blog/intimacy-path-toward-spirituality/201506/why-pride-is-nothing-be-proud.

Amundson, Greg. *The Warrior and the Monk: a Fable about Fulfilling Your Potential and Finding True Happiness.* Robertson Publishing, 2018.

Barker, Kenneth L., et al. *NIV Study Bible New International Version.* Zondervan Publishing House, 2011.

Becker, Joshua. "The Life-Freeing Nature of Forgiveness." *Becoming Minimalist.* June 19, 2014, www.becomingminimalist.com/the-life-freeing-nature-of-forgiveness/

Braime, Hannah. "Your Resentment Is a Message. Are You Listening?" *Becoming Who You Are.* August 8, 2016, www.becomingwhoyouare.net/blog/resentment-message-listening.

Byrne, Rhonda. *The Secret.* Atria Books, 2018.

Buggy, Patrick. "The Upstream Solution: Treat the Source of Your Problems, Not the Symptoms." *Mindful Ambition.* November 29, 2018, www.mindfulambition.net/upstream-solution.

Chapman, Gary D. *The Five Love Languages: How to Express Heartfelt Commitment to Your Mate.* Northfield Publishing, 2004.

Chopra, Deepak. *Seven Spiritual Laws of Business Success.* Rider, 1998.

Christopher Cross. "Ride Like The Wind." *Christopher Cross*, Warner Bros. Records, 1980.

Dawson, Loenie. *2015 MY SHINING YEAR BIZ WORKBOOK.* BenBella Books, 2015.

Dyer, Wayne W. *Wisdom of the Ages: a Modern Master Brings Eternal Truths into Everyday Life.* HarperCollins Publishers, 1998.

"Early Childhood Development Overview." Unicef data, www.data.unicef.org/topic/early-childhood-development/overview.

Sommer, Elle, et al. "4 Steps to Stop Feeling Guilty When You've Done Nothing Wrong." *Live Purposefully Now.* May 7, 2020, www.livepur-posefullynow.com/4-steps-to-stop-feeling-guilty-when-youve-done-nothing-wrong/.

Elrod, Hal. *The Miracle Morning: the Not-so-Obvious Secret Guaranteed to Transform Your Life before 8AM.* 2016.

Emmons, Henry and Rachel Kranz. *The Chemistry of Joy.* Fireside, 2006.

Emmons, Henry. *The Chemistry of Joy: a Three-Step Program for Overcoming Depression through Western Science and Eastern Wisdom.* Fireside, 2006.

Firestone, Lisa. "Dealing With Unresolved Trauma." *Psychology Today*, Sussex Publishers,  March 28, 2018, www.psychologytoday.com/ca/blog/compassion-matters/201803/dealing-unresolved-trauma.

Gilbert, Elizabeth and Mireille Vroege. *Big Magic: De Kunst Van Creatief Leven.* Cargo, 2016.

*International Journal of Medical and Health Research.* www.ijmhr.org.

James, John W. Grief Recovery Handbook. Harper Perennial, 1998.

Kralik, John. 365 *Thank Yous: The Year a Simple Act of Daily Gratitude Changed My Life.* Hyperion, 2015.

Manson, Mark. *The Subtle Art of Not Giving a f*Ck: a Counterintuitive Approach to Living a Good Life.* Harper Paperbacks, 2019.

MC Hammer. "2 Legit 2 Quit." Capitol Records, 1991.

National Domestic Violence Hotline. "Get Help Today: 1-800-799-7233." April 8, 2020. www.thehotline.org/.

Needtobreathe. "Hard Love." Atlantic Records, 2016.

Mayo Clinic, Mayo Foundation for Medical Education and Research. "Post-Traumatic Stress Disorder (PTSD)," July 6, 2018, www.mayo-clinic.org/diseases-conditions/post-traumatic-stress-disorder/symp-toms-causes/syc-20355967.

Priebe, Heidi. *The Comprehensive INFP Survival Guide.* Thought Catalog Books, 2016.

QuickRead and Kondo Marie. *The Life-Changing Magic of Tidying up: The*

*Japanese Art of Decluttering and Organizing: Summary and Analysis*. CreateSpace Independent Publishing Platform, 2015.

Ruane, Jessica. "How to Let Go of Resentment and Anger." *Lifehack*, March 5, 2020, www.lifehack.org/articles/lifestyle/how-to-let-go-of-a-resentment.html.

Rubin, G. *The Happiness Project*. HarperCollins, 2015.

Rugged Maniac. *Rugged Maniac 5k Obstacle Race & Mud Run*, www.ruggedmaniac.com.

Ruiz, Miguel. *The Four Agreements: a Practical Guide to Personal Freedom*. Amber-Allen Publishing, 2017.

Sheena Easton. "Strut." *A Private Heaven*, EMI America, 1984.

Sincero, Jen. *You Are a Badass: How to Stop Doubting Your Greatness and Start Living an Awesome Life*. Running Press, 2017.

Survivor. "Is This Love." *When Seconds Count*, Scotti Bros., 1986.

Tolle, Eckhart. *The Power of NOW: a Guide to Spiritual Enlightenment*. Namaste Publishing, 2004.

Mtsho, BsTan 'dzin rgya, and Howard Cutler. *The Art of Happiness: A Handbook for Living*. Yellow Kite, 2017.

www.ingramcontent.com/pod-product-compliance
Lightning Source LLC
Chambersburg PA
CBHW030826090426
42737CB00009B/889